Hope on the Brink

Hope on the Brink

Understanding the Emergence of Nihilism in Black America

LEWIS BROGDON

With a Foreword by Stephen Ray Jr.

CASCADE *Books* · Eugene, Oregon

HOPE ON THE BRINK
Understanding the Emergence of Nihilism in Black America

Cascade Books
An Imprint of Wipf and Stock Publishers
199 W. 8th Ave., Suite 3
Eugene, OR 97401

www.wipfandstock.com

ISBN 13: 978-1-62032-757-9

Cataloguing-in-Publication data:

Brogdon, Lewis.

Hope on the brink : understanding the emergence of nihilism in black America / Lewis Brogdon ; with a foreword by Stephen Ray Jr.

xii + 94 pp. ; 23 cm. Includes bibliographical references.

ISBN 13: 978-1-62032-757-9

1. United States—Race relations. 2. African Americans—Social conditions. 3. African American churches. I. Title.

B185.615 .B725 2013

Manufactured in the U.S.A.

Contents

Foreword by Stephen Ray Jr.   *vii*

Acknowledgments   *xi*

Introduction: My Encounter with
Nihilism   1

One   The New Face of Nihilism   15

Two   The Internalization of Racial
           Oppression   33

Three   Nihilism and the Prospects of Social
           Annihilation   53

Four   Nihilism and the Crisis of Black
           Religion   69

Bibliography   91

Foreword

Hopelessness and despair are perhaps the most vicious hounds unleashed to dog the steps of humanity. For while it is yet true that war, pestilence, genocide, and catastrophe regularly visit suffering upon us, more often than not this is for a season. Where devastation occurs there is the still capacity to envision new fields, new homes, new lives— new hope. Where hopelessness and despair reign, however, there is little more than the ashen fields salted with the bitter tears of broken dreams. Where in the instance of catastrophe persons and communities can be rebuilt, with bone-deep despair and hope little more than a memory there is but survival. This is the stuff of nihilism; put simply, survival in the absence of hope. As many commentators have observed, this is one of the particular evils which besets the black community in the late modern era. While there have been any number of works in social scientific and theological literature about this tragic situation, there have been few works that have comprehensively detailed the nature and contours of the matter as well as this work.

In the pages that follow Lewis Brogdon explores the idea of nihilism with a nuance and depth that is sorely needed in the church today. The reason I use a term broader than he (the church) to talk about the value of this work is that the problems with which the book grapples are ones facing the church, as such. One of the great tragedies of the modern era has been the general abandonment of critical and sustained engagement by the church with the "least of these." A consequence of this abdication has been that it has largely been left to the black church to confront and be witness to life in the face of death-dealing systems born and given continued life by the historical and contemporary manifestations of racism. So, the timeliness of this text is both for the black church and for the church, as such, if it is to fulfill its vocation as the Body of Christ to the *whole* of God's creation.

Beyond its timeliness, this book also provides an important account of the enduring and seemingly intractable conditions of cultural marginalization and economic exclusion that bedevils so many communities. Too often it is the case that commentators on the plight of impoverished communities proceed as if the problem is with malformed communal attitudes and practices, rarely taking notice of concrete material conditions which create a fertile ground for perduring despair. As Brogdon notes, the root causes of the nihilism that he describes is sustained economic exclusion. This point cannot be overstated. In a society such as ours in which one's humanity and dignity are inextricably linked to participation in the economic system, non or limited participation has serious consequences. It would not be an overstatement to suggest that what we are dealing with here is contemporary form of what Orlando Patterson described as "social death."[1] After all, in a consumerist society where one's identity is wrapped tightly with the capacity to consume and the character of one's consumption, what does it mean to be financially incapable of consumption beyond the barest essentials as the continual state of one's life? One becomes a non-person. Before moving on it is well to note

1. Patterson, *Slavery and Social Death: A Comparative Study* (Cambridge: Harvard University Press 1985).

that the intergenerational character of this economic exclusion is perhaps the most pernicious dimension of the life conditions that give rise to nihilism. As Brogdon notes, one can find witness to this throughout the decades. One has but to reread the Kerner Commission Report on Civil Disturbances written in 1968 and note how little has changed for members of economically disadvantaged portions of the black community to see this reality.[2]

The enduring nature of this situation creates particular challenges for those who seek to address the despair and nihilism to which it gives rise. Here again, this work does a masterful job of plumbing the depths of this challenge. An image that I often use to describe the situation is this: it is like working in an emergency room and a shooting victim is wheeled in and you begin triage with a daunting challenge; the perpetrator is still shooting the victim even as you work. This image is particularly apt because so often gun violence is the most visible manifestation of the nihilism about which Brogdon writes. So, the challenge is more than simply developing means to deal with communal trauma as a memory—a mistake that many make when talking about the legacy of slavery and segregation. The issue is dealing with a historically traumatized community, while simultaneously interpreting and responding to continuing traumatization. With this understanding the magnitude of issues with which this book deals becomes clear.

While I find myself more in agreement with Derrick Bell about the intractability of problem[3]—my Calvinist inclinations I suspect—the underlying presumption of this work, that something can be done even if it is tentative and

2. *Report of the National Advisory Commission on Civil Disorders* (New York: Bantam, 1968).

3. Bell, *Faces at the Bottom of the Well: The Permanence of Racism.* (New York: Basic, 1993).

temporary is compelling. It is in a way the mirror opposite of nihilism. That is to say, hope becomes the final word; a hope that is undaunted by the seeming endlessness of adversity. As it rightly point out in the text this hope is at the core the black Christian witness through these last few centuries. It is not Nietzsche's hope of the weak, nor is it misplaced hope of Fred Price. Rather, it is the hope which has animated the Christian faith from its very beginnings. It is the hope that perennially reiterates the infinite value that God has ascribed to each and every person and the fullness to which it destines them, in spite of the continuing negation of it by the forces of a fallen world. In the end, this is nature of the struggle against nihilism, the struggle for hope.

In closing, let me say what an honor it is to write this preface to a truly fine piece of scholarship and ecclesial reflection on a significant issue. I have known Lewis since he began his Master's studies more than decade ago. This has allowed me to watch, and hopefully participate, in the development of a promising scholar and churchman. I have very faith, largely validated by this work, that his is a voice that will contribute significantly to the shape of theological discourse in coming decades and to making it relevant to the needs of the black church and community.

Stephen G. Ray Jr.
Neal A. and Ila F. Fisher Professor of Theology
Garrett-Evangelical Theological Seminary

Acknowledgments

I WOULD LIKE TO thank my family, friends, and colleagues
for all the support they have given me over the past three
years. I have been preoccupied and focused on understanding nihilism in black communities and without your support, love, encouragement, and wisdom I would not have
completed this project with hope that change is possible.
I want to dedicate this book to my beautiful, intelligent,
fun, loving, and gifted children: Sarah, Charity, Micah,
and Daniel. Thank you for sacrificing time we could've
spent together so I could write this book. Your generosity
has made this possible. I am tremendously blessed to be
your dad and hope that in some way, this book makes the
world a better place for you and your children. I want to
thank the love of my life, Mrs. Felicia Quire-Brogdon, for
her love and encouragement. Thanks for the coffee and the
listening ear as I talked about this project. I want to thank
my mother Rev. Earleen Brogdon and my sisters, Lois,
Christina, Stephanie, Marsha, Laurie, Linda and my broth-
er-in-laws Bob and Keith for continuing love, laughs, and
good food. My mom and deceased father Lewis Brogdon
Sr. taught my sisters and me the value of faith in God, hard
work, and education. I want to thank my mentors Bishop
Fred Brown, Dr. Derrick L. Miles, and Dr. Estrelda Alexander. You model professional excellence with deep care
for people. My life, ministry, and scholarship are so much

better because of you. I also want to thank Dr. Stephen Ray, Dr. Johnny Hill, Rev. Darvin Adams, Rev. Jeremy Franklin, Julius Crump, Rev. Elizabeth Shannon, Dr. Elizabeth Zagatta-Allyson, and Amanda Brack for various contributions toward the completion of this book. Lastly I want to thank my colleagues at Louisville Seminary, especially my colleagues in the Black Church Studies Program, and the Trinity Presbyterian Church in Dayton, Ohio for the opportunity to serve as a professor and church leader.

"Now unto him that is able to do exceedingly abundantly above all that we ask or think, according to the power that works in us" (Ephesians 3:20).

My Encounter with Nihilism

THIS BOOK IS AN attempt to explore a phenomenon that emerged from my work as a minister in African American churches in Virginia, West Virginia, and Kentucky. Serving as a pastor of inner-city and rural congregations, I became increasingly aware of an internal apathy that seemed to be eating away at people like a cancer. What I observed was not just the frustration or resentment resulting from a lack of access to opportunities non-blacks are often afforded, but a deeper problem—one encompassing a kind of pervasive spiritual, psychological, and emotional despair, and anger. I witnessed African Americans who were resigned to accept the status quo instead of working for change. I witnessed African Americans who, ironically, possessed a deep suspicion and hatred of their own culture and people. I witnessed African Americans who ignored, actively resisted, and sometimes undermined programming and leadership who were working to improve black communities. I also witnessed young people who lacked self-esteem alongside the desire to expand their minds and chase educational opportunities that promise life success. Worse yet, I witnessed too many funerals for young black men and women. While many died as victims of violence at the hands of other African Americans, some tragically chose to end their own lives.

What was so troubling to me about the passivity, self-defeating actions, destructive lifestyles, and violence that I encountered was that these behaviors and attitudes worked against the change so desperately needed in the African American community. Instead of challenging injustice and working for change, I watched black people—young and old—resign themselves to the belief that this was the way of the world. They were content to survive with little to no motivation to thrive. Accepting injustice as the norm, participating in undermining one's own community, and committing acts of violence were counterproductive responses from persons within the black community who were deeply frustrated, sad, depressed, and angry. My experience ministering to these individuals and communities was a wake-up call for me to a pervasive problem that I soon discovered had not gone unnoticed. After serving on panels with community leaders and engaging in conversations with African American pastors across ten states, it became increasingly evident that others in the black community were confronting the same reality and searching for ways to understand it.

MY SEARCH FOR UNDERSTANDING

In varying ways, the perennial question that leaders in black communities have asked throughout the first decade of the twenty-first century is "what's wrong with black America?" The National Urban League, for example, publishes annual reports that chronicle the "State of Black America" on issues such as education, voting rights, health care, poverty, incarceration rates, home ownership, and the many disparities faced by African American women, in particular. During this decade, Tavis Smiley invited African American leaders from across the nation to convene an annual conversation on the state of black America. These spirited and illuminating discussions touched on many of the issues identified by the National Urban League's reports, offering probing analyses that sought to deepen the nation's understanding of the plight of African Americans. The panels were aired on C-SPAN and often followed up with books that attempted to offer guidance for addressing various social problems.

As each year passed, the best and brightest leaders in black America tried to wrap their minds around the persistent and pervasive problems tearing at the fabric of our communities. They educated the nation about the plight of the African American community, arguing that even during years of great prosperity many blacks were still negatively affected by the legacy of slavery and racism. It was apparent to me that the real value in these panel discussions was that they helped the United States to think deeply and critically about the problems vexing black America. The conversations also revealed to me and others that the problems plaguing the black community are extremely complex, perhaps unable to be explained simply by the legacy of slavery and ongoing racism.

Popular books and scholarly studies also sought to address the problems plaguing African American communities. For example, Tom Burrell's book *Brainwashed* asks hard questions like "why can't we build strong families, why do we perpetuate black sexual stereotypes, why do we keep killing each other, why do we keep killing ourselves, and why can't we stick and stay together?" As his title suggests, Burrell argues that blacks have been brainwashed and that the myth of black inferiority is the reason blacks participate in lifestyles that undermine their community and a healthy sense of self. Similarly, Matthew Ashimolowo's *What is Wrong with Being Black,* Bill Cosby and Alvin F. Poussaint's *Come On People,* sociological studies such as John Mc-Whorter's *Losing the Race,* and William Bennett, John Dilulio and John Walters's *Body Count* all attempt to address the ways black people are hurting themselves. They expose behaviors and attitudes prevalent in the black community that drive up mortality rates among African Americans and contribute to the increasing number of blacks in the criminal justice system. Worse yet, these behaviors and attitudes not only affect how African Americans live and love, but they also reinforce many of the racial stereotypes that blacks have been fighting for centuries.[1] Though these works name and adequately explore the issues affecting blacks, they fail to provide a language or a conceptual framework that helps us to understand *why* blacks are doing these things. What is it that causes blacks to turn against themselves?

Beverly Tatum and Cornel West gave me the language I needed to explore this phenomenon. In a discussion of racial stereotypes, Tatum mentions how members of a stereotyped group "internalize the stereotypical categories about his or her own group."[2] She refers to this as internalized oppression. Instead of rejecting racial stereotypes, blacks who internalize racism accept them and live with a distorted vision of oneself, one's community, and the world. These persons will no doubt influence their families and communities in harmful and sometimes destructive ways. Using Tatum's language of *internalized oppression* is one way to understand the destructive turn against self and

1. Burrell, *Brainwashed*; Ashimolo, *What Is Wrong With Being Black?*; McWhorter, *Losing the Race*; Bennett, Dilulio, Jr., and Walters, *Body Count.*

2. Tatum, *Why Are All the Black Kids Sitting Together in the Cafeteria?*, 6.

community in many African American communities. But *nihilism* was the term that best captures this struggle in the black community. Cornel West was the first to use the term for African Americans. Others would follow, such as Bakari Kitwana, Homer Ashby, Amos Wilson, and Reginald Davis, each contending that nihilism is the best way to interpret the unique constellation of problems in black communities.[3] I share this belief. Thus, this book joins the conversation about the plight of black America and our future.

I believe that the black community is on the brink of hopelessness and meaninglessness because of the increasing numbers of African Americans who participate in their own oppression. Like West and others, I am convinced that the fragmentation and decline affecting black communities is a sign of nihilism. What the term nihilism attempts to identify in this case are not just social inequities linked to historic racism. Rather, nihilism also signals the toll racism has taken on black communities, including the adoption of self-defeating lifestyle choices that ultimately worsen their plight.

Take, for example, the following statistics on education: Only 12 percent of African American fourth graders have reached proficient or advancement reading levels, while 61 percent have yet to reach basic reading levels. Similarly, many black seventeen-year-old students graduating high school have the math skills of their white counterparts who are just finishing up the eighth grade. Part of what I am suggesting is that understanding educational deficiencies like these must factor in not only the structural forces that ensure blacks attend subpar schools, but also the growing

---

3. West, *Race Matters*; Kitwana, *The Hip Hop Generation*; Wilson, *Blueprint for Black Power*; Ashby, *Our Home Is Over Jordan*; Davis, *The Black Church*.

number of blacks who themselves devalue the importance of education and do not strive to learn.

Racism explains the former challenge, while the latter, I believe, is influenced by nihilism. Let me further tease out this distinction. On the one hand there are many young blacks who want a quality education but are not afforded the opportunity and must settle for subpar schools and poor teachers. This lack of access to a quality education is a product of inequities linked to racist and discriminatory practices. On the other hand, there are young blacks who attend good schools and have access to a good education, yet these young people are content to be undereducated or, worse yet, to drop out of school altogether. In other words, there are scores of young blacks with access to textbooks and quality teachers who *choose* not to better themselves and resultantly set themselves on the path to poverty and unemployment. In this latter instance, the young blacks who refuse to apply themselves in school or drop out of school altogether demonstrate an internal apathy that I am identifying as nihilism. There is something amiss in the spirits and minds of these young people, as well as many others in black communities, that is worthy of further exploration and understanding.

Nihilism gives language to the increasing numbers of blacks who set themselves up for failure. They do so because they have internalized their oppression. Internalized oppression recognizes the myriad ways in which blacks are turning on themselves and their communities, living out a self-defeating and, at times, a self-destructive way of life. Nihilism best explains the despair, animosity, resentment, violence, and other reckless forms of thinking and behaving rampant in some black communities. Nihilism is not only encountered and recognized by religious leaders like myself, but also by school teachers, community leaders, political leaders, law enforcement officers, and the citizens living in black communities across the nation. What has become increasingly clear to me, through my work with pastors and church and community leaders, is that black America has a serious problem that is pushing hope for the African American community to the brink of despair and meaninglessness.

I in no way mean to suggest that all African Americans are nihilistic. Historically African Americans have been pathologized and blamed for their unjustified enslavement, segregation, and discrimination. I am trying not to pathologize African Americans. But I believe it is important for every community to be open to self-examination and self-critique, even communities that have experienced oppression. However, such examinations and critiques must be done understanding the issues and challenges unique to this history. Assessing the plight of the black community is a delicate issue that must take into account the impact of the history of racism, respect the agency of blacks to organize their lives and world, and reflect an ability to think critically about both external and internal issues affecting the black community. In my work, I strive to balance these issues. Nihilism's emergence in the African American community is intimately related to the history of slavery and racism in the United States. I do not underestimate the impact of this history. However, I choose not to victimize African Americans, but rather respect the agency of blacks and, consequently, focus on how internalized racism drives some African Americans to use their agency in harmful ways. In this sense, my goal is to show that nihilism is a pervasive problem affecting many in the black community.

Nihilism is a product of centuries of racism and emerges as a result of its sustained presence and lingering effects. In a time when the President of the United States is

African American and when so many African Americans are wealthy, successful, and celebrated by many in this country, it is hard for some to believe that racism is still a problem. In fact, some people contend that we are living in a post-racial era. There is no doubt that racism is a polarizing issue in this country. On one hand, there are people who adamantly refute any claim that there is racism in this country. They may even claim that blacks use the race card as an excuse for their refusal to take responsibility for their own actions and communities. To them, any appeal to racism is only an attempt on the part of blacks to avoid the hard work requisite for success. On the other hand, there are people who believe that America has not made any progress with racism and because of this conclude that every problem in the black community is linked to racism. There are even some people who believe that most whites are still deeply racist persons who secretly hate blacks. There are differing opinions about racism and also confusion. I am often surprised by the ignorance and misinformation that fuels people's opinions and beliefs of this important subject.

Therefore, it is important to clarify two matters: what I mean by racism and the different ways it affects African Americans. What do I mean by racism? My understanding of racism is heavily influenced by the work of Beverly Tatum. Her classic study of racial identity entitled *Why Are All the Blacks Kids Sitting Together in the Cafeteria?* was one of most influential books I read in seminary. Tatum introduces what I believe is the most common misunderstanding about racism, which is the belief that it is solely prejudice. For many, when they hear racism, they are thinking about racial prejudice. She defines prejudice as preconceived judgments or opinions, usually based on limited information, and says that everyone has prejudices, not because they want them, but rather because everyone is exposed to misinformation. She adds, "Prejudice is one of the inescapable consequences of living in a racist society."[4] Even though prejudice is a consequence or manifestation of racism, it is important to understand that prejudice is not the same thing as racism.

Tatum argues that it is better to understand racism as a system of advantage based on race. Great emphasis should be given to the idea of racism as a system and not just prejudicial beliefs. Racism persists because it is enforced and reinforced by systems. White Americans benefit from a system of advantage rooted in centuries of slavery and legalized discrimination. So when African Americans claim they are victims of racism, many of them are thinking systemically and not necessarily about prejudicial beliefs. They are thinking about the history of racism and how it concretizes privilege and inequality.

During the two-plus centuries of slavery, the political, economic, and social infrastructure of this country was built. This infrastructure was set up to benefit whites while excluding and taking advantage of blacks, who were legally given little access or altogether shut out of the system. For example, between 1862 and 1936, the United States government granted 1.6 million homesteads, approximately 270 million acres of federal land given for private ownership. One study of inequalities found that these Homestead Acts, "provided up to 160 acres of land, self-reliance, and ultimately wealth to millions of Americans families."[5] Thomas Shapiro notes that the number of homestead descendants living today at 46 million adults, which means "that up to a quarter of the adult population potentially traces its legacy of property ownership, upward mobility, economic

4. Tatum, *Why Are All the Blacks Kids Sitting Together in the Cafeteria?*, 6.

5. Shapiro, *The Hidden Cost of Being African American*, 190.

stability, class status, and wealth directly to one national policy—a policy that in practice essentially excluded African Americans."[6] This system benefits whites, giving them "access to better jobs, schools, housing, even when they do not embrace overtly prejudicial thinking," but disadvantages blacks and is why blacks continue to experience significant social challenges.[7] Racism is best understood in the systemic sense and Tatum's work is helpful in highlighting this important dimension to racism.

So what do I mean when I say that nihilism is the product of racism? I am stating that racism linked to slavery and legalized segregation has led to the establishment of systems that continue to discriminate against and disadvantage blacks. These systems are racist because of the economic, political, and social inequities they produce, where whites are at the top and blacks are on the bottom. Over time, the systemic form of racism takes a toll on the black community and the emergence of nihilism is an intricate part of the cumulative toll of racism.

When people in this country see successful African Americans, such as Barack and Michelle Obama, Oprah Winfrey, Robert Johnson, Tiger Woods, Michael Jordan, Toni Morrison, T. D. Jakes, and Maya Angelou, the temptation is to believe racism is not hurting African Americans. I would contend that racism is a significant factor for the African American community even though much has changed in black America over the past four decades. African Americans are not experiencing racism in the same way, which is why it is important both to recognize the diversity in the black community and the ways some segments are more vulnerable to nihilism than others. Studies on the African American community often speak in broad

6. Ibid., 190.
7. Ibid., 7.

sweeping terms when referring to African Americans such
as "the black community," "the African American community," or "black America," without giving attention to the
tremendous amount of diversity that these terms represent.
Eugene Robinson challenges the practice of clumping all
blacks together by arguing desegregation has effectively
dis-integrated or splintered blacks into four broad groups
or categories. He categorizes black America as consisting of

> a mainstream middle class majority with a full
> ownership stake in American society; a large,
> abandoned minority with less hope of escap-
> ing poverty and dysfunction than at any time
> since Reconstruction's crushing end; a small
> transcendent elite with such enormous wealth,
> power, and influence that even white folks have
> to genuflect; and two newly emergent groups—
> individuals of mixed race heritage and commu-
> nities of recent black immigrants.[8]

His description of black America allows us to recognize
the progress that has been made in the past four decades
by African Americans. But it also allows us to recognize
the large numbers of blacks who continue to face significant challenges. He maintains that a large segment of the
black community is "languishing in poverty" and have
been "abandoned with no way out of poverty and social
dysfunction." While it is important to recognize that there
are highly successful and wealthy African Americans, that
should not distract us from focusing on the broader context
of black America where many continue to suffer devastating disadvantages linked to racism. I hope to demonstrate
that the very diversity we celebrate as evidence of racism's
decline is actually an indicator of a pervasive nihilism that
threatens the fabric of black communities and America.

8. Robinson, *Disintegration*, 5.

HOPE ON THE BRINK

You will find that my first chapter is historical in nature, introducing the works of Friedrich Nietzsche and Cornel West to examine the meaning of the word nihilism and its emergence in Europe in the nineteenth century and in African American communities today. Next, I explore the application of nihilism in the African American community in what I refer to as *The New Face of Nihilism*. I maintain that slavery and racism produce a different kind of nihilism from that which Nietzsche encountered in Europe. This chapter goes on to provide a brief history of the emergence of nihilism in black America, beginning in the late seventies and continuing through the first decade of the twenty-first century. The increasing presence of poverty and unemployment in black communities contrasted with the success of white Americans, reaping the benefits of an emerging global economy, are key precursors to the emergence of nihilism. After developing a working understanding of the historical context for nihilism's emergence, I explore the impact of nihilism on African Americans individually and communally.

In chapter 2 I define and discuss my understanding of nihilism as *The Internalization of Oppression*. Here, the reader finds considerable attention given to the psychological toll of racism. A nihilistic mindset emerges from the considerable toll racism has exacted on blacks and thrives on the members of the black community who are unable to hold up under its weight and strain. This leads to a number of blacks who internalize their oppression. In particular, they internalize despair, self-hatred, and inferiority. But the story of nihilism's emergence surpasses its influence on the individual; we must also account for the impact of nihilism in the communal sphere. I take up the self-destructive tendency of nihilism in the context of community in the third chapter entitled, *Nihilism and the Prospects of Social Annihilation*. When blacks internalize racism, a new form of Social Darwinism emerges, pitting blacks against one another, fostering increased racial hostility toward non-blacks, and breeding a fundamental disregard for others. Perhaps nihilism's most dangerous expression is captured by those blacks who, in their own words, "don't give a fuck"—a sentiment which boldly proclaims that they do not care about themselves or others.

My final chapter examines *Nihilism and the Crisis of Black Religion*. In the same way that racism has taken a considerable psychological toll on blacks, it has also taxed their spirits and religious institutions. For centuries, blacks turned to religion to figure out how to live, love, and flourish in the midst of racism and discrimination. Religion has given language to African Americans as they suffered the horrors of slavery. Religious practices like singing and prayer provided ways to express both despair and hope. And religious institutions such as churches have provided safe spaces for communal expression and organization. But to-day many African Americans are slowly turning away from and abandoning religion. To illustrate this, I explore some of the recent critiques leveraged against the black church. In particular, I examine the critiques that the black church is disconnected from the social realities affecting the black community because churches are too preoccupied with entertainment and containment. Some are turning away from the black church because they believe it has turned on them. What these critiques are missing is the nihilistic impulse driving some blacks to "feel good" religion. "Feel good" religion may act as a temporary salve, but, in the end, it fails to give meaning to the complex questions religious blacks bring to their communities of faith. Religious beliefs and practices that do not address the deep angst and hope-lessness experienced by many in the black community only feeds the nihilism that pushes the black community to the brink. Black religion must take up the challenge of nihilism with beliefs and practices that can genuinely lead to healing and the renewal of hope and meaning. *Hope on the Brink* is not a book offering anecdotes and quick fixes. In the pages that follow, I seek to provide an interpretation of nihilism that will continue the conversation about the plight of black America, and spur further study about the effects of racism, as well as advocacy by activists and religious leaders.

One

The New Face of Nihilism

HISTORICALLY, BLACKS HAVE STRUGGLED in America, but today something is different. Something is deeply wrong in the black community today. The problem in the African American community is not just the continuing presence of social injustice and economic inequities, but rather a growing internal apathy and spiritual emptiness in the eyes and minds of too many in the black community. This apathy expresses itself in hopelessness and meaninglessness and results in self-defeating and self-destructive lifestyles. For example, Randall Robinson, a former Harvard University law professor, links problems like high infant mortality, low income, high unemployment, substandard education, capital incapacity, insurmountable credit barriers, high morbidity, below average lifespan, and over-representation in prison and death to what he calls "a disabling poverty of means and spirit."[1] In other words, what troubles black America is a combination of both structural inequities and a deeper internal apathy that I've come to recognize as a new form of nihilism.

---

1. Robinson, *The Debt*, 62.

NIHILISM: FROM EUROPE TO BLACK AMERICA

Friedrich Nietzsche wrote about nihilism in nineteenth-century Europe. He believed that a crisis had begun in Europe and would last for two centuries. The crisis Nietzsche envisioned was the emergence of nihilism. Nietzsche is often associated with atheism but his ideas on nihilism, though not as popular or well understood, are important. For him, nihilism was rooted not only in the failure of foundational beliefs and values to give meaning to the world but also the realization that universal beliefs and values were fabricated to substantiate the status quo of the powerful. These foundational beliefs were intricately tied to the dominance of Christianity in the West. He said, "The time has come when we have to pay for having been Christians for two thousand years."[2] The Christian interpretation of the world, as a universal and true depiction of reality, was collapsing along with the values and morals undergirding it. In its wake, a radical nihilism emerges that claims everything is false and results in deep skepticism and pessimism as a new posture toward any sense of the universal in the world. Nihilism in its mild form challenges the moral interpretation of the world and in its more radical forms challenges the belief that there is any meaning in the world and beyond the world. Nihilism's rise was not just a rejection of all beliefs and values, but the inadequacy of such beliefs to address the pressing existential questions of the time. Contrary to the belief that all forms of nihilism lead to annihilation, for Nietzsche, the acceptance of the belief that there is no order and meaning in this life does not lead to chaos but rather the attempt to construct a world that gives meaning. At its core, nihilism is a rejection of a set of beliefs that fail to give

2. Nietzsche, *The Will to Power*, 20.

meaning and hope to lived realities. The nihilistic turn can take different trajectories: resulting in the pursuit of alternate meaning or the rejection of meaning itself, which can result in social anarchy, withdrawal, and violence.

Nietzsche's understanding of nihilism provides a helpful beginning point for this study for two reasons. First, even in the late nineteenth century, he believed that nihilism would be a part of human history for the next two centuries. His focus was on nihilism in Europe but nihilism will emerge in America. During the time of his writings in the nineteenth century, blacks in America were struggling to forge a future as free persons after centuries of slavery. The plight of blacks and their struggle in America will prove to be a substantial part of nihilism's history in America. In a manner similar to Nietzsche's claim that the time had come when Europeans would pay for having been Christians, it appears that the time has come for a self-designated "Christian" nation to pay for building a wealthy democracy while killing, enslaving, and discriminating against Native and African Americans. And the toll appears to be a moral and social crisis that poses formidable problems for this nation. Nietzsche also underscored the fact that the demise of any system of beliefs, values, or a society's ability to make sense of life leads to nihilism—the rejection of a world of meaninglessness and the choice either to pursue an alternate world of meaning or to undermine the present social order. Therefore, to some extent, nihilism can be present in all societies and is not a reality confined to nineteenth-century Europe. For these reasons, Nietzsche provides a valuable blueprint to examine the social fragmentation and internal malaise so prevalent in African American communities today. What Nietzsche's work does not address is the kind of nihilism that emerges when the beliefs and values tied to a social system have been linked to centuries of slavery and discrimination on the basis of race. In contrast to nihilism in Europe, any form of nihilism in America will invariably have to account for centuries of racism. This issue serves as a starting point for a study of nihilism's emergence in black America.

The first to view nihilism as a major issue in the black community was Cornel West. African American leaders have examined the plight of the black community in sociological studies and books of varied kinds. West's work is important because it uses the term *nihilism* to interpret the crisis of hope and meaning that has emerged as a result of racial oppression. For West, the emergence of nihilism is the appropriate way to interpret the plight of the black community and the unique challenges that emerge as a result. In *Race Matters,* he identifies the despair that manifests itself in communities across America. He says,

> To talk about the depressing statistics of unemployment, infant mortality, incarceration, teenage pregnancy, and violent crime is one thing. But to face up to the monumental eclipse of hope, the unprecedented collapse of meaning, the incredible disregard for human (especially black) life and property in much of black America is something else.[3]

For West, the real issue confronting black America is not merely structural inequities, as the liberals argue, or lack of morals and work ethic, as the conservatives would contend, but rather the "profound sense of psychological depression, personal worthlessness, and social despair" that is widespread in black America.[4] He does not use the term *nihilism* in the same manner as Nietzsche. Instead, West uses the term to describe the collapse of meaning and social

3. West, *Race Matters*, 19.
4. Ibid., 20.

upheaval that results from cultural buffers that broke under the weight of centuries of racism. In the wake of broken buffers a pervasive nihilism emerges in a growing number of blacks who confront the "lived experience of coping with a life of horrifying meaninglessness, hopelessness, and love-lessness" and results in a growing number of blacks with a "numbing detachment from others and a self-destructive disposition toward the world."[5]

Nihilism's emergence is the result of fractured social safeguards and cultural buffers. For West, facing nihilistic conditions is not new for Americans of African descent because slavery and segregation posed similar threats. However, the current nihilistic threat poses a formidable challenge because the social or cultural buffers in place to protect the African American community from the onslaught of racism have now been fractured, leaving the black community vulnerable.

Diagram 1

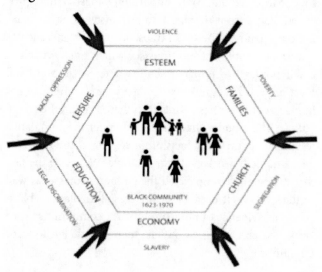

---

5. Ibid., 23.

What the above diagram attempts to illustrate is how cultural buffers insulate the black community from racism. As a marginalized group, the African American community constructs buffers to ward off marginalization's destructive and dehumanizing effects. For example, blacks developed buffers that provide a healthy sense of esteem and identity. In these communities, people who were called nobodies were told they were somebody. Without the buffers, there was a real possibility that larger numbers of blacks would have internalized the belief of being a nobody. Members of these communities emphasized the importance of faith, family, education, leisure, and economic independence as ways to counter the effects of slavery, segregation, and legal discrimination. Churches and families were particularly instrumental in constructing buffers that led to strong communities and institutions with holistic persons in a racist culture. For centuries, these buffers kept nihilism at bay and protected countless lives from the evils racism sought to carry out. More importantly, these buffers protected blacks from slipping into responsive behaviors and lifestyles that become social traps. Social problems such as poverty, unemployment, crime, substance abuse, violence, and illiteracy are problems buffers attempt to ward off. West argues that nihilism's emergence and entrenchment in black communities is linked to these fractured cultural buffers. These buffers have fractured under the cumulative weight of centuries of racism. Once strong, these buffers have gradually weakened. For example, West says the fact that young black people lead the nation in suicide, as well as the level of self-hatred that often results in black on black crime, as evidence of nihilism. In black communities with weakened and fractured buffers, there is little left to ward off nihilism.

In sum, the work of West proves that nihilism is an important part of any assessment of the African American community today and demands new paradigms, beyond the typical liberal and conservative models. In addition to this, his work is important for the three reasons that will inform the present study. First, West frames the emergence of nihilism within the larger context of racism in America and its continuing effects. For him, nihilism is linked to racism. Second, nihilism provides language that enables us to understand the despair, internal angst, and deterioration that fuels the continued decline of the black community in the post civil rights era. Third, nihilism is a helpful way of understanding why some blacks are locked into counter-productive and destructive behaviors and lifestyles. There is considerable value for using nihilism as a lens to interpret the plight of the African American community. But more attention needs to be given to nihilism as a response to institutional racism and nihilism as internalized oppression.

THE NIHILISTIC TURN

What Nietzsche and West describe are responses to a crisis of meaning. The responses occur in different historical eras and social contexts. But it is important to emphasize that nihilism is a response to a crisis within a historical or social context. In Europe, the crisis was tied to Western Christian beliefs and values losing their ability to help some people make sense of the world. In America, for blacks, the crisis is tied to slavery and racism. The response to the crisis of the times is what I identify as the nihilistic turn. The nihilistic turn is the decision to reject as senseless prevailing beliefs, ideologies and practices that exploit, dehumanize, and destroy human thriving. People turn from prevailing beliefs, ideologies and social practices to nothingness (Latin *nihil*).

But also, the racialized form of nihilism in America gives blacks the burden of trying to make sense of racism, the persistence of racism, and the grinding power of racism. Over time, this exacts a considerable spiritual, psychological, and social toll that leads to an eventual breakdown of a substantial number of black institutions and persons. Because of this breakdown, many blacks internalize racial oppression, in particular, internalizing despair, self-hatred, and inferiority. Once racial oppression is internalized, blacks participate in their own oppression, thereby sustaining the power and permanence of racism. Much of the social isolationism, black on black crime, political, social, moral irresponsibility, and religious chicanery of prosperity preaching and entertainment preaching are examples of the nihilistic turn and ways blacks are now hurting themselves and their respective communities.

THE EMERGENCE OF NIHILISM
IN BLACK AMERICA

While nihilism is the result of centuries of slavery and institutional racism, its emergence is a byproduct of three decades of grinding poverty and economic decline. These dual factors provide a proper historical backdrop from which to understand nihilism's emergence. A large segment of the black community began to experience significant decline in the decades following the Civil Rights movement. These decades will give rise to a crisis that will affect blacks as the promises of equality and hopes generated from the civil rights movement fade into obscurity by the early nineties. Economic decline from the mid-seventies onward, with stifling poverty and unemployment, set the stage for nihilism's emergence. This struggle with poverty and lack of access to economic opportunities will take a major toll on black communities over the next three decades, unleashing a pervasive despair and anger that America saw glimpses of after the assassination of Martin Luther King, Jr. The despair and anger abated but would later manifest itself.

During the eighties and nineties, the level of social deterioration increased, rapidly leaving black communities across the nation vulnerable. For example, transnational corps and mega-corporations took manufacturing jobs away from urban centers to suburbs and overseas. According to sociologist Douglas Glasgow, these developments had a devastating effect on black youth, which Glasgow refers to as the black underclass in his study. His assessment is startling.

> Over the past fifteen years, the nation's inner cities have witnessed the growth and consolidation of a population of poor and unused Black youth, confined to economic poverty and social decay. A significantly younger population than the poor of previous generations, these young blacks, some as young as thirteen or fourteen, are already earmarked for failure—they are undereducated, jobless, without salable skills or the social credentials to gain mainstream life. They are rendered obsolete before they can even begin to pursue a meaningful role in society.[6]

Glasgow's assessment demonstrated the social decay on the rise in the seventies that became widespread in the eighties. During this time, hundreds of thousands of blacks were left in poverty and largely unemployed. For example, in 1982 the unemployment rate for blacks was 18.9 percent, which was twice the 8.4 percent rate among whites. In 1985, the unemployment rate for blacks was 16.3 percent compared

6. Glasgow, *The Black Underclass*, vii.

to 6.2 percent among whites.[7] Two terms utilized in the study that reinforce the dire conditions are *entrapped* and *underclass*. Regarding this large groups of black youth, he describes them as "a permanently entrapped population of poor persons, unused and unwanted" that has "accumulated in various parts of the country."[8] Drawing on the language of classism and specifying large groups of blacks as an underclass is a particularly helpful way of situating my understanding of nihilistic conditions. These dire conditions will have a profound effect on this group of blacks as they come of age over the next few decades. Coupled with rising unemployment, black youth were left to seek economic opportunities through selling drugs and other illegal means, which Bakari Kitwana refers to as the underground economy.[9]

African Americans also turned to religion to combat the economic decline of the seventies and eighties. In particular, they turned to a form of religion that promised material prosperity. Prosperity preaching churches took root in black inner city churches during this time and flourished as disenfranchised blacks sought economic empowerment and opportunities from God and religious enterprises. In the eighties and nineties, Fred Price introduced and popularized prosperity teaching in the black community. Price was born in Santa Monica, California in 1932 and was the eldest son of Winifred and Fred Price. His formative years were spent in Los Angeles. Price's educational accomplishments included graduating from Dorsey High School, receiving an Associate degree from Los Angeles City College, and later receiving an honorary doctorate from Oral Roberts University, in Tulsa, Oklahoma. Currently Price serves

7. Franklin and Moss, *From Slavery to Freedom*, 570.
8. Glasgow, *The Black Underclass*, 3.
9. Kitwana, *The Hip Hop Generation*, 13.

as pastor of Crenshaw Christian Center in Los Angeles, with a membership over twenty thousand. His television broadcast *Ever Increasing Faith* airs in fifteen of twenty of the largest markets in America reaching more than fifteen million households per week. Dr. Price provides spiritual oversight to over three hundred churches through a network called the Fellowship of Inner City Word of Faith Ministries (FICWFM—founded in 1990). Through this ministerial network and television broadcast, Price popularized prosperity teaching in inner cities. Other African American pastors, most of which were in Pentecostal, Neo-Pentecostal, or Neo-Charismatic churches, taught prosperity in urban centers across the country, feeding the megachurch boom. Large numbers of African Americans were particularly drawn to churches with this emphasis on material prosperity. These developments—poverty and unemployment and the turn to crime and or religion—are revealing factors about the social context of this time and a pervasive desire to escape these dire realities.

The appeal to the underground economy and prosperity religion during this time was so tempting because of the increasing number of wealthy Americans. The decade of the eighties was not only a story about poverty and unemployment among a large segment of black America, but also about wealth that was largely inaccessible to poor blacks. During this time, "the rich got richer and the poor got poorer."

> In 1980 there were 574,000 millionaires in the United States. Eight years later, there were 1.3 million Americans who were millionaires. In 1981 there were a mere handful of billionaires, but by 1988 there were at least fifty-two. Put another way, the average per capita income of the top 1 percent of Americans increased from $270,000 in 1977 to $404,500 in 1988.

> Meanwhile the average per capita income of
> the lower 10 percent fell from $4,113 in 1977 to
> $3,504 in 1988.[10]

Witnessing this kind of wealth and lacking proper means to access it will be a significant factor in the animosity and resentment that fuels nihilism. What is particularly significant about this is that the majority of blacks during this time fall in the lower 40 percent in income, which means they were not benefitting from the explosion of wealth. Furthermore, increased wealth only widened the inequality gap between whites and blacks and served as a poignant reminder that blacks were falling further behind economically and socially.

Thomas Shapiro argues that the wealth gap is the key to understanding racial inequality. Shapiro's research proves that wealth is the real measure of racial inequality and not income or wage disparities. Whites have both wealth and income, enabling them to leverage opportunities and overcome hardships in ways blacks cannot since they only have income. Because blacks are asset poor, they are commonly susceptible to poverty as evident by the fact that nine of ten African Americans will encounter poverty during their working adult years.[11] Yet on the other hand, whites have that safety net, because of the bump given them from the economic boom they experienced in the Reagan years, and went into the decade of the nineties financially stable in ways working and poor blacks were not. Shapiro states, "One reliable source estimates that parents will bequeath $9 trillion to their children between 1990 and 2030."[12] His study found that the richest 1 percent of families controls

10. Franklin and Moss, *From Slavery to Freedom*, 576.

11. Shapiro, *The Hidden Cost of Being African American*, 6–8, 32–37.

12. Ibid., 5.

38 percent of total household wealth, and the top 20 percent controls 84 percent. They also own "47 percent of the value of stocks, bonds, real estate, businesses, and other financial instruments, and one-fifth of America's families controls 93 percent." Furthermore, the "top 20 percent receives about 42 percent of all income while the "financial wealth of the bottom two-fifths of the population actually falls into negative numbers," meaning debts overshadow assets.[13] Family wealth, according to Shapiro, cancels gains in classrooms, workplaces, and paychecks, and compounds racial inequality.

The recession of the early nineties and the ever widening gap between upper- and middle-class whites and a large black underclass, trapped in a vicious cycle of poverty, proved to be difficult for many blacks. Black communities felt the brunt of the recession of the early nineties and languished. These conditions were ripe for nihilism to flourish. And these conditions gave rise to rampant despair and violence. Kitwana characterized these decades as "a time of drive-by shootings, homelessness, gang wars, and extreme poverty in urban communities."[14] As communities continued to decline, a growing number of blacks turned to violence. While studies of the black community during the eighties and nineties invariably address the increase in violent crime, they miss the deeper connection to nihilism. The turn to violence betrays a deeper anger than a flat read of statistics on crime. Instead it signals a nascent nihilism on the rise that would only worsen as conditions did not improve as the decade concluded.

At the end of the decade of the nineties, things went from bad to worse for a large number of blacks. Former President Bill Clinton commissioned a study on race that

13. Ibid., 44.
14. Kitwana, *The Hip Hop Generation*, 129.

would provide a broad look at both the progress made by racial ethnic people as well as the challenges they continue to face. According to the study, the progress made by African Americans during the early twentieth century was slowed and even reversed between the mid-1970s and early 1990s.[15] The study covered population, education, labor markets, economic status, health, crime and criminal justice, and finally housing and neighborhoods. In all areas, African Americans continue to suffer significant disadvantages. This presidential study demonstrated that the plight of the African American community at the turn of the century and into the first decade of the twenty-first century had taken a turn for the worse. This report only stated on paper realities that blacks had been facing for over two decades. With so many advances lost and failed promises linked to the civil rights movement, there was cause for real concern about the plight of black Americans.

Beyond the dire social conditions represented in the report, these losses arouse lingering doubts and anger from the bitter years leading up and through the Civil Rights movement. The movement, as representative of the work of Dr. Martin Luther King, Jr., symbolized the quest to live in a society where all citizens, black and white, have access to opportunities for success. Regardless of the conflict the movement caused among blacks, there was a general consensus that the aims were beneficial—making things better for blacks. The legislation and other benefits that came as a result of the movement cost many their lives, most notably Martin Luther King, Jr., which resulted in a backlash of violence and rioting in major cities. His death symbolized a potential threat to hard-earned gains that he and others worked for on behalf of others. In a similar manner to his

15. Council of Economic Advisors for the President's Initiative on Race, *Changing America*, 13–32, 40–41, 60–68.

death, the presidential report that Civil Rights gains were being lost aroused deep feelings of despair and anger.

Three decades of social and economic decline and the accompanying demise of hope in what the Civil Rights movement could do for all African Americans unleashed nihilism. Two points bear mentioning. First, it is clear that these social conditions were having a cumulative effect on the psychological, emotional, and physical well-being of African Americans. Second, there is a connection between dire social conditions, counterproductive responses by blacks to dire social conditions, and the emergence of nihilism. Black scholars and leaders writing on nihilism invariably address the intersection between the social conditions of the black community, the responses to these conditions, and nihilism.

Homer Ashby, a black pastoral theologian, describes the current condition of the African American community as being engaged in not only a struggle for freedom, justice, and equality but also a struggle for survival.[16] The term *survival* reflects the accelerated rate of social decline that the black community continues to experience, as seen in the aforementioned presidential study commissioned in 2000 on racial equality. The plight of African Americans is dire because of the severe state of fragmentation that threatens the collective survival of blacks in America. Ashby provides two examples to support his belief and in the first example he alludes to the influence of nihilism. Black on black crime is both a threat to black communal survival and a vestige of nihilism. He suggests the blacks who kill other blacks participate in a "mental and physical process whereby (they) internalize the oppression they experience" and express those feelings through violence.[17]

16. Ashby, *Our Home Is Over Jordan*, 13.
17. Ibid., 7.

One notable target of this practice was Rosa Parks, the civil rights icon, who was assaulted in her own home in Detroit by a member of the black community who even recognized yet disregarded her. It has been estimated that over 90 percent of those who murder, rape, and assault black people are black people themselves.[18] Second, Ashby cites a study on hypertension in the black community that found that "the emotional states of depression and hopelessness contribute significantly to high blood pressure" and that "black Americans are two or three times as likely to develop hypertension and at age twenty-five are twice as likely to have high blood pressure as their white counterparts."[19] Studies on depression rates among African Americans and hypertension are indicators of a deeper problem. Both examples make a correlation between social problems like poverty, responses to these problems such as black on black crime and hypertension, with nihilism. It is apparent the rise in nihilism among African Americans is not only threatening communities with violence but is also impacting the emotional well-being of blacks.

In conclusion, Friedrich Nietzsche wrote about nihilism in the nineteenth century believing that it would not only plague Europe but also the world for the next two centuries. Nihilism, as a crisis of purpose and hope in belief and values that are unable to give meaning to human experience, manifests itself in a unique way in America for persons of African descent who experienced centuries of slavery and then legalized segregation and discrimination. Cornel West made the connection between nihilism and

18. Hine, Hine, and Harrold, *The African American Odyssey*, 627.

19. Ashby, *Our Home Is Over Jordan,* 5. Cited study by Davidson, Jonas, Dixon, and Markovitz, "Do Depression Symptoms Predict Hypertension Incidence in Young Adults in the CARDIA Study?" *Archives of Internal Medicine*, 1495–1500.

the social fragmentation latent in the African American community. For West, nihilism affects a growing number of African Americans who experience a life that lacks meaning, hope, and love. As a result, these blacks undermine their own community and participate in various forms of violence from murder to suicide. This response, that I call the nihilistic turn, is rooted in the history of racism and the presence of racism today. What I am suggesting is that some blacks are turning away from the meaninglessness and hopelessness of a country that continues to oppress and discriminate against them and an abusive and destructive power that still claims the lives of too many blacks to isolationism, violence, pleasure, and a religion that inoculates them from the pain of this world. In the pages to follow, I will explore this nihilistic turn as one response among many to racial oppression.

Two

The Internalization of Racial Oppression

RACIAL OPPRESSION EVENTUALLY BREAKS psychological defenses in individual persons as well as broader social buffers. The experience of being "broken" underscores not only the physical toll of racial oppression, as evident by the countless number of beatings enslaved Africans suffered during slavery and the lynchings of the Jim Crow years, but also the psychological and emotional toll of experiencing forced subjugation through violence and unjust laws. Racism's story in America is not just about physical violence and force. It is also about the psychological and emotional beatings African Americans have endured and continue to endure, the countless numbers of blacks who broke under this weight, and the undercurrent of nihilism that arises as a result. I turn my gaze to the internal thought world of blacks and what it means to internalize their oppression.

THE PSYCHOLOGICAL TOLL OF
RACIAL OPPRESSION

In the 1903 classic work *The Souls of Black Folk*, W. E. B. DuBois asked "How does it feel to be a problem?" That question began what would become one of the more significant insights into the inner thought world of blacks. For DuBois, living in a racist society produces an internal struggle in the soul. Concerning this struggle, he says it is,

> a peculiar sensation, this double-consciousness, this sense of always looking at one's self through the eyes of others, of measuring one's soul by the tape of a world that looks on in amused contempt and pity. One ever feels his two-ness,—an American, a Negro; two souls, two thoughts, two unreconciled strivings; two warring ideals in one dark body, whose dogged strength alone keeps it from being torn asunder.[1]

DuBois's characterization gives insight into the internal struggle that blacks feel in their soul as they seek to reconcile the experience of being black in a country that dehumanizes and excludes people of African descent from full participation in society. Countless blacks can attest to the experience of double-consciousness.

Double-consciousness, the feeling of alienation and not belonging, is acutely felt and produces internal turmoil as one seeks to reconcile this feeling with the desire to belong and contribute to society. This concept is appropriate for this study because it gives insight into the internal dimensions of racial oppression, particularly that the experience of oppression produces an internal struggle in the soul. DuBois's last statement about the "dogged strength" required to keep one's soul from being torn asunder is

1. DuBois, *The Souls of Black Folk*, 9.

especially relevant because it raises the possibility that a failure to hold together these unreconciled strivings can lead to nihilism. Because of the nihilistic possibility, blacks struggle to claim a healthy sense of identity.

THE BREAKING POINT

Systemic racism that is sustained over time eventually breaks individual persons and groups of people to the point that it is easier to subjugate them. To illustrate this point, I will draw on the memory of an enslaved African, William Colbert, who discussed the violent beating of a slave named January. The memory was so vivid because of what it did not only to January but also the effect it had on others. It graphically illustrates the purpose of oppression, which is to break the internal defenses and well-being of persons and communities.

> So when brother January he come home, de massa took down his long mule skinner and tied him wid a rope to a pine tree. He strip his shirt off and said: Now nigger: I'm goin to teach you some sense. Wid dat he started layin' on da lashes. January was a big, fine lokkin' nigger; de finest I ever seed . . . when de massa begin a beatin him, January neber said a word. De massa got madder and madder kaze he couldn't make January holla. What's de matter wid you, nigger? He say. Don't it hurt? January he neber said nothin' and de massa keep a beatin till little streams of blood started flowin down January's chest, but he neber holler. His lips wuz a quiverin and his body was a shakin but his mouf it neber open; and all de while I sat on my mammy's and pappy's steps a cryin. De niggers wuz all gathered about and some uv em couldn't stand it; dey

> hadda go inside dere cabins. Atter while, Janu-
> ary he couldn't stand it no longer hisself, and he
> say in a hoarse loud whisper: massa massa hve
> mercy on dis poor nigger.[2]

There is no doubt that this marked a significant turning point in January's involuntary servitude. The resistance he formerly clung to was beaten out of him by the master. He tried to resist but under those conditions he eventually broke and more than likely accepted the existing social arrangement, abuse and all, as normative. In other words, "This is the way it is and this is the way it is going to be." Being forced to accept this reality is a significant setback and influences the personal and communal development of blacks. Too often accounts of the African American struggle frame the history based on January's defiant resistance. There is some value in this kind of portrayal. But this is by no means the whole story, because though January resisted, the beating continued until he broke.

This is the nature of oppression and its ultimate telos (purpose)—for blacks to be forced to accept that this is the way it is, this is the way it is going to be, and there is nothing they can do to change it. The historical context of the oppressor may change but the oppression remains. In other words, the experience of January is not confined to the whipping post but is reenacted in different ways. African Americans from the days of slavery, Reconstruction, and Jim Crow segregation, to the men today who are victims of the prison industrial complex and the black women who receive less income for more work, all have their own experiences of breaking under the weight of racial oppression. Racial oppression not only imposed physical injury but also psychological injury that continues to impact individuals and communities in different ways. In fact, the

2. Berlin et al., *Remembering Slavery*, 24–26.

psychological toll of oppression and the subtle, blatant breaches in black attempts at resistance is an important factor behind the emergence of nihilism.

INTERNALIZED OPPRESSION

There is an additional dimension to the psychological toll of racism that studies commonly overlook. Blacks struggle to resist a systemic racism yet some adopt or imitate racist ways of being from their white social counterparts. Blacks not only suffer as victims of racism but are socialized into racist ways of thinking and living through what Rene Girard calls a "mimesis of apprenticeship" (*mimetism primaire*).[3] Mimesis, which means imitation, representation, or mimicry, refers to the process of imitation that is a base part of human socialization. When mimesis happens in America, blacks imitate or mimic the evil of racism they are exposed to by whites. Some blacks reason that if whites pour racial hatred upon them, then they, in turn, should respond by pouring racial hatred back on to whites. Some Black Nationalist groups, though well intended, attempt to instill a sense of pride in blacks, but often only mimic the evil of white supremacy. This dehumanizes blacks and argues that they are inferior by producing a form of black supremacy that dehumanizes whites and makes whites inferiors to blacks.

Joy D. Leary's provocative text *Post Traumatic Slave Syndrome* uses trauma studies to examine the ways blacks continue to be affected by the legacy of slavery. One of the traumatic effects of slavery and its racist underpinnings is what she describes as "racist socialization."[4] When this

3. Girard, *Deceit, Desire, and the Novel*, 7, 15.
4. Leary, *Post Traumatic Slave Syndrome*, 139.

happens marginalized, oppressed or "captive persons take on views and attitudes of captors" and also adopt the "slave master's value system."[5] Leary describes a type of mimesis. Her description of racist socialization is not merely blacks imitating racist practices of their white counterparts but rather mirroring or reflecting the evil of racism in different yet destructive ways. The example she used was the belief that all things associated with whites are superior to all things associated with blacks. Blacks, through mimesis, imitate this belief. But Leary comments that it produces inferiority among blacks. When this happens, blacks are reflecting the belief in white superiority in ways that lead them to view themselves as inferior. The foundation of the master's values is the belief that whites are superior to blacks. She argues that blacks internalize this belief and as a result mirror inferiority, affecting how they see themselves and how they relate to fellow blacks and whites.

It is here that the difference between European nihilism and African American nihilism is most evident. In America, blacks suffer as victims of oppression but also in some instances internalize or mirror racial oppression. The internalization or reflection of oppression produces a form of nihilism different than what emerges in Europe. What it produces are a substantial number of African Americans who manifest despair, self-hatred, and inferiority in a profound way. This mimesis of racial hatred only darkens the mind and spirit of blacks and as we will see in this and the next chapter, unleashes a nihilism that contaminates the spirit and community. I will examine the constituent elements of the nihilism that breaks the spirit of individual blacks.

5. Ibid., 139.

DESPAIR

Nihilism's first element begins by internalizing despair. In particular, nihilistic despair rests on the belief that it is impossible for America to change its racist and discriminatory ways. It is, therefore, hopeless to believe that resisting racism improves the plight of African Americans. This belief unleashes a kind of despair that is more severe than what Cornel West suggests. Nihilistic despair is not merely the loss of hope but is actually the result of the *death of hope.* Hope is not lost in many black communities, it has died.

Hope's death happens in stages. First, nihilism is the product of centuries of racial oppression and continuing social inequities. Racism expresses itself not only by dehumanizing practices and ideologies, but also by exploiting and marginalizing blacks in a capitalistic system. American capitalism and wealth is inextricably linked to centuries of slave labor and a political and legal system that solidified an unjust social arrangement guarantying that European Americans economically benefitted from these oppressive and exploitative social practices. Today, many blacks feel hopeless or struggle to maintain hope as they attempt to assess why they are still largely lagging behind their white counterparts. One of the difficult realities about the post-Civil Rights African American community is the fact that in spite of the progress made in the last forty-plus years, the African American community as a whole is facing difficult and in some instances dire social conditions.[6] The fact that African Americans comprise only 12.4 percent of the U.S. population yet remain at the bottom of economic and social indicators like education, employment, health, and housing is discouraging to a number of blacks.

6. Muhammed, "Race and Extreme Inequality"; Pinkney, *The Myth of Black Progress.*

The second stage shifts from the experience of anomie to how some African Americans interpret the continuing inequities and disparities. African Americans, from Harvard-trained law professors to the men and women in community barbershops and beauty salons, believe that discrimination and inequality will forever permeate American society. The belief that America is fundamentally and irreparably broken is central to Black Nationalist sentiments that go back to the first enslaved Africans who resisted oppression and integration and continue to evidence themselves in groups such as the Nation of Islam, the Black Panthers, and African American churches such as Trinity United Church of Christ in Chicago.[7] The variations of this belief helps interpret or make sense of the social disparities. For example, in *Faces at the Bottom of the Well*, Derrick Bell offers political and legal perspective on racial discrimination. He argues that American history is a clear indicator that racism will be permanent in America. Historically, democracy and racism inherently reinforce one another, Civil Rights gains and other social advancements will be temporary, and setbacks are inevitable. In this sense, African Americans will experience a never-ending

7. See Lincoln, *The Black Muslims in America*; Asante, *An Afrocentric Manifesto*; Cone, *Martin and Malcolm in America*; and Washington, *Black Sects and Cults*, 20–21. These works investigate the nature of Black Nationalism in African American history and also discuss other beliefs and resultant responses such as integrationist or accommodationist traditions that hold to a fundamentally different belief about America's history and its responses to racism. Moreover, Washington identifies African dimensions of this belief in what he calls "the tradition of fatalism" that claims the power to affect the affairs of human belongs to God. For him, black cults are able to resist oppressive realities because the tradition of fatalism locates power and control over human affairs with God. This interpretive move then informs the nature and function of cultic worship that seeks to be empowered to participate in shaping alternative social realities.

cycle of advancements, setbacks, advancements, and setbacks. His belief contrasts with the belief that America can overcome racism. Inequities exist because America lacks the fundamental will to change the social construction of society. As such, history is a reminder of the intentional choice America made to build society by including some and excluding others. History is not only an indication and but also a guarantee of the continuation of racial inequality in the present. This country's history of slavery is what he describes as a "legacy of enlightenment from our enslaved forbearers" reminding us if they survived the ultimate form of racism then we can survive its many contemporary forms. In other words, he believes that "what has always been will always continue to be" in new and more pervasive forms. Bell adamantly argues,

> Black people will never gain full equality in this country. Even those herculean efforts we hail as successful will produce no more than temporary peaks and progress, short-lived victories that slide into irrelevance as racial patterns adapt in ways that maintain white domination. This is a hard-to-accept fact that all history verifies. We must acknowledge it, not as a sign of submission, but as an act of ultimate defiance.[8]

What Bell is articulating is the belief that racism is a permanent fixture on the American landscape and that social (structural) inequality is a reality that people of African descent, in varying ways, have to accept as normative, without conceding the struggle for equality. Bell wants to liberate blacks from living with the myth that racism will end; instead he wants to arm blacks with realism as they fight racism—that will always be—in America.

8. Bell, *Faces at the Bottom of the Well*, 12.

The third stage in this process is both complex and painful. There are many blacks like Bell who believe America will not change its racist and discriminatory ways. However, unlike Bell, this belief for some others does not inspire defiance but rather despair because of what appears to be a losing battle. A growing number of blacks question what is the purpose of fighting this losing battle or resisting the inevitable. Historically, African American leaders who resisted racial oppression and challenged injustice often lost their lives. King dreamed, but was killed. The same can be said for other leaders, especially the countless numbers of black women whose suffering buoyed black social advancement. Both their lives and deaths advanced the black cause for justice and equality. Yet some advancements were seemingly, short-lived and seemingly benefitted some, but not all, African Americans. Such advancement, many times with great sacrifice and even death, and often with a later loss of ground, fails to inspire a growing number of blacks to continue resisting, and instills a sense of hopelessness. In the face of fighting a losing battle, hope slowly dies. And today, the black community is increasingly populated by people whose hope in a just and equitable society either died a long time ago or continues to die as they face stifling social inequities and disappointing economic disparities.

I heard a similar comment while teaching a study on why the church struggles with the issue of racism. One older congregant from the Civil Rights generation said, "We already heard that and tried that. Nothing has changed." Instead of working for change, some blacks, like this congregant, choose to respond to the permanence of racial inequality by retreating from the struggle altogether, accepting the inequitable nature of society as permanent, after having one's hope die a slow, painful death. Despair, which is the death of hope, precedes nihilism's second expression, the descent into self-hatred.

SELF-HATRED

The second and more enigmatic element of nihilism is self-hatred. Self-hatred is one of the often ignored and yet persistent products of racism. Unfortunately, there are a growing number of African Americans, even very successful ones, who harbor a deep disdain of their blackness and or African identity, hating the reality that they are African American in a European American context. Two twentieth-century thinkers witnessed self-hatred. In *The Luminous Darkness*, Howard Thurman assessed the internal toll of living in a segregationist society. He found that one of the unfortunate vestiges of racial separatism was self-hatred.

> The real evil of segregation is the imposition of self-rejection. It settles upon the individual a status which announces to all and sundry that he is of limited worth as a being. It rings him round with a circle of shame and humiliation. It binds his children with a climate of no-accountness as a part of their earliest experience of the self. Thus it renders them crippled, often the length and breadth of their days . . . I think this is the root of what seems to be the careless regard that Negroes sometimes have for their own lives and the lives of their fellows. It is extraordinarily difficult to see day after day your life and the life of your fellows cheaply held, to be born and to live in the midst of a climate of violence without being affected by it . . . Life cheaply considered in the environment tends to cause those whose lives are so regarded to deal with their fellows in ways that reflect the same attitude.[9]

Thurman shows how the shame and humiliation of racism robs blacks of self-love and self-esteem, causing blacks to

9. Thurman, *The Luminous Darkness*, 24–25.

view themselves as less than human. For Thurman, this leads to self-hatred.

Malcolm X was notorious for his critiques of white America. I believe the significance of his thought was in his beliefs about how blacks could better their condition while combatting the evils of racism. He believed that blacks should be united and in order to accomplish this self-hatred must be confronted with self-love.[10] For him, internal dissension and strife within the black community were evidence of a lack of self-love. The fact that blacks lacked the self- and communal love required to work for change was highly problematic. He also believed the underlying reason for counterproductive behaviors among blacks was conditioned self-hatred. And for him, such self-hatred emanated from black people's ignorance of their history and culture on one hand, and believing white ideological views about blacks on the other. In the wake of ignorance and misinformation, blacks are socialized to inevitably despise themselves.[11] His beliefs are so important because they were rooted in a vision of new ways blacks and whites could relate to one another. Malcolm X believed that until blacks stopped hating themselves and resultantly began loving themselves, they could not authentically relate to others.

As in the sixties and seventies, self-hatred is still present in the African American community. A recent CNN story on American children and race illustrates the socialization of self-hatred that reaches even the youngest and most vulnerable. In this study, children were questioned regarding which skin color they preferred, which skin color was ugly or bad, which child was ugly, etc.[12] Surprisingly,

10. Cone, *Martin and Malcolm in America*, 105–6.

11. Woodson, *The Miseducation of the American Negro*.

12. http://ac360.blogs.cnn.com/2010/05/17/ac360-series-doll-study-research/.

many black children repeatedly pointed to the lighter skin tones as preferable, with one child commenting that brown skin looks "nasty" sometimes.[13] In a similar manner, Kelly Brown Douglas's insightful study, *Sexuality and the Black Church*, found that blacks struggle with self-hatred as it relates to their bodies and sexuality, which complicates how they relate to themselves and others.[14] Both studies highlight the influence of socialization as it relates to black self-hatred. In the bold and compelling text, *The Debt: What America Owes Blacks*, Randall Robinson identifies what this CNN study documented as self-hatred. In simple and yet profound words, he states that today "not all but too many" African Americans hate themselves.[15] Like Malcolm X, Robinson connects self-hatred to a collective ignorance of two important elements: the history of Africans in America from enslavement to today and African history and culture before American enslavement.[16]

Yet self-hatred is not only connected to African Americans' ignorance of history and culture; it is also connected to the painful and unresolved nature of the history of slavery in America. African Americans remain conflicted about their understandings of this history, its significance for today, and the value of remembering slavery as a resource

13. http://i2.cdn.turner.com/cnn/2010/images/05/13/expanded_results_methods_cnn.pdf.

14. Douglas, *Sexuality and the Black Church*.

15. Robinson, *The Debt*, 83.

16. Cone, *Martin and Malcolm*, 105. Malcolm told an audience in Philadelphia that blacks are a lost people with no knowledge of their name, language, homeland, God, or religion. He added that other people no matter where they live know where they come from, except the "so called Negroes," who think they are Americans. His point demonstrates how ignorance hampers blacks' ability to form a healthy sense of identity that fosters agency and causes blacks to rise and work for change.

to illumine contemporary issues in the black community. Robinson argues that ignorance fuels contemporary forms of self-hatred. I would contend that historical ignorance is not just the source of self-hatred but also the plethora of conflicting thoughts and feelings about slavery. There is ambivalence, shame, anger, resentment, and a profound sadness regarding this history in the black community.

There are some blacks who believe we have done this to ourselves, which feeds self-hatred. I characterize this as the turn against oneself. Robinson describes it accordingly, "We [blacks] don't know what has happened to us and no one will tell us. Thus we have concluded that the fault must be ours. We blame and disparage ourselves but seldom those responsible for our dilemma."[17] Without historical and cultural knowledge, blacks are left to internalize blame that feeds self-hatred. In this way, historical ignorance and misinformation feeds the nihilism rampant in black communities. Robinson further explains that this history causes a crushing loss of confidence among blacks themselves. The description of the loss of confidence among blacks is intricately connected to accepting or internalizing the belief that blacks are inferior. As a result, he notes, blacks who accept this belief follow a downward spiral to self-hate, self-disparagement, and anger. In light of many African Americans who are ignorant and or conflicted about their history in America, a vacuum is created that is eventually filled with animosity directed toward oneself, which expresses itself in unfortunate ways including self-degradation, imitation of white culture, violence against oneself, violence against other blacks, and communal degradation.[18]

17. Robinson, *The Debt*, 83.

18. Lincoln, *The Black Muslims in America*, 34–36. Lincoln mentions self-hatred as a minority group's response to living in an environment of prejudice and discrimination. However, self-hatred was

INFERIORITY

Nihilism's second component, self-hatred, is connected to the third component, which is the internalized belief in the inferiority of blacks. Ultimately some blacks hate themselves because they think they are nobodies, "social nothings." In contrast to the religion of some blacks that imparted a sense of somebodiness, blacks who have become nihilistic internalize a sense of nobodiness. Inferiority is a byproduct of the history of slavery and racism. The belief in the inferiority of blacks was an important belief employed by whites in the eighteenth and nineteenth century to justify slavery. Katie Cannon argues, "To justify (African) enslavement, Black people had to be completely stripped of every privilege of humanity" and were resultantly divested "of all intellectual, cultural, and moral attributes."[19] Cannon believes that it was important to view blacks as a sub-par species between animal and human in order to satiate the conscience of a nation practicing one of the grossest forms of enslavement in human history. This belief not only serviced to justify slavery but also the belief was an important doctrine in the segregation era so as to justify separating blacks from whites and subjugating them. Persons of African descent in America were indoctrinated by whites for centuries to believe in the inferiority of Africans. White Americans drew on racist teachings about African people to buttress their belief from major Western intellectuals. Consider David Hume's statement that he "suspects the Negroes . . . to be naturally inferior to the white. There never was a civilized nation of any other complexion other than

---

an expression of avoidance. His discussion of avoidance as a response to racial oppression sheds some light on my understanding of the nature of self-hatred.

19. Cannon, "Slave Ideology and Biblical Interpretation," 120.

white, nor even any individual eminent either in action or speculation."[20] Founding Father Thomas Jefferson, sub-scribed to this belief as well, saying, "Comparing them by their faculties of memory, reason, and imagination, it appears to me that in memory they are equal to the whites, in reason much inferior, as I think one could scarcely be found capable of tracing and comprehending the investigations of the Euclid; and that in imagination they are dull, tasteless, and anomalous."[21]

According to these influential Western thinkers Africans are naturally inferior to whites. Beyond the absurdity of such statements, the real issue is what happens in the spirits and minds of blacks who internalize or accept these beliefs. Since the days of slavery on through to the educational system of today, blacks have not only been referred to as inferior and less than human by whites but also to varying degrees have been taught to think of themselves as inferior and to accept this belief. Historical studies of African Americans document the many blacks who resisted and countered the doctrine of black inferiority. But again, not all blacks rejected this belief. Some accepted it. And today, there is a segment of the black community that has internalized the belief in the inferiority of blacks.

For blacks lacking social and spiritual safeguards that provide a healthy sense of self, some are left to accept the belief that the reason blacks continue to suffer is because they are inferior to other races and cultures. Inferiority, once internalized, affects blacks in a myriad of ways from self-disparagement to defeatism. Inferiority has a dual effect on blacks and only serves to strengthen the nihilistic

20. Hume, *Essays and Treatises*. Cited in J. E. Harris, *Africans and their History*, 19.

21. Jefferson, "Notes on the State of Virginia." Cited in Robinson, *The Debt*, 50.

hold it has on them. Blacks believe they are inferior on two levels: the ontological and the social. They individualize the belief that, at the core of their being, they are inferior. And they believe that not only are they inferior but most if not all their black counterparts are inferior as well. This internalized belief only feeds the self-hatred previously discussed. But it also manifests itself in a very unique manner in black America. Internalized belief in black inferiority is largely responsible for the increasing numbers of blacks who disparage blacks and practice self-defeating behaviors.

Randall Robinson recalls an experience of listening to a black comedian disparage and degrade black persons, a trend that is widespread among African American comedians. As he sat through the routine, what he called a saddening spectacle, he asked himself, "What accounts for such self-degradation?" For him, not only is historical ignorance about black culture the culprit, but also "a pervasive global belief that blacks are inherently inferior."[22] For him, self-disparagement is a reflection of a pervasive sense of shame rooted in the belief that blacks are inferior people. Self-disparagement masks not only self-hatred but shame. When understood this way, one could say blacks disparage and laugh at themselves in an attempt to keep from crying. Nothing reinforced the influence of inferiority like my time as a pastor among rural and inner city black youth. I found that youth have internalized inferiority and live with a deep sense of shame, which has a devastating effect on their lives. I encountered numerous young blacks who, for example, refuse to project their voice when speaking in public, are unable to speak clearly, and even mumble when you talk to them. Often these young people, particularly young black boys, walk with their head down. I was repeatedly saddened by the number of young persons who devalue education

22. Robinson, *The Debt*, 85.

and actually think it is cool to be uneducated and ignorant. Instead of just expressing my dismay to the persons practicing these self defeating lifestyles, I sought to understand what was behind this. I asked myself, could it be possible that some young blacks who are unable to clearly speak do so because they believe they don't have anything of value to say? I also pondered if some under-perform in school on purpose because they don't believe they are intelligent in the first place. What I witnessed among black youth is the product of internalizing the belief that blacks are inferior. And youth are not the only members of the black community to internalize this belief. It pervades all segments of black America from the successful ones who are constantly trying to prove themselves to whites (and themselves) that they are not inferior, to the ones society deems unsuccessful and accept that belief, living a life of underachievement and mediocrity.

Nihilism is not just a crisis of dire social conditions but the story of an increasing number of blacks who respond to these conditions in counterproductive ways. Instead of social inequality, the focus of this chapter has been on the internal dimensions of racial oppression. Racism takes a considerable psychological toll and over time breaks the spirit and has caused the deaths of millions of blacks. In contrast to the belief that blacks keep on struggling until they overcome, the real intent of racism is to break the spirit of blacks so they accept oppression as their lot in life. The reality is that some struggle until their strength, hope, and faith dies. While historians of black America valorize the ones who survived racism's onslaught, there is another piece to this history that is often ignored—those who broke under the weight of racism and lived in misery.

In every respect, the experience of breaking under this weight is a crisis of meaning. The experience of losing hope and being forced to accept an unjust world has a devastating effect. Blacks are forced to construct a world of meaning with injustice as its foundation and center. Historically, there have been some who created a positive world of meaning for themselves and others. However, there has been a mass of blacks unable to construct a positive narrative but instead internalize their oppression and draw from it ways to give meaning to the world. For example, instead of resisting the culture of racial violence, some blacks value and practice violence against others and themselves. Studies on the African American community have expressed concern for this troubling trend but few have delved into the psyche and spirits to understand internalized oppression: the death of hope, the persistence of self-loathing, and the pervasive belief that blacks are inferior. These components produce a destructive nihilism that tears the fabric of black communities. The communal effect is just as important as the internal dimensions. Now we will turn from the inward gaze into the souls of black folk experiencing nihilism to its effects on the broader community.

Three

Nihilism and the Prospects of Social Annihilation

IN THE BOOK *The Black Church*, Reginald Davis describes the present state of the black community as a community in crisis. Davis, writing with a sense of urgency, compels the black church to address the current state of crisis.

> To say black America is in deep spiritual, psychological, social, economic, and political trouble is an understatement. Our crisis is so critical that if we don't appropriately act against systemic oppression and the appalling apathy it produces in the oppressed, then black America will continue to disintegrate, which is a frightening and despairing reality for the future.[1]

For Davis, hope is on the brink in black America. He argues that if action is not taken, disintegration and despair will characterize the future of too many in the African American community. His statement illustrates the real concern for the broader community by a growing number of African American religious leaders, over the counterproductive

1. Davis, *The Black Church*, 6.

attitudes and lifestyles as well as the increase in violence in black communities. It also reveals a deeper concern and possible fear that if things continue to deteriorate our future will be negatively affected. Davis raises the prospects of social annihilation for many in black America.

Nihilism not only breaks down individual blacks with despair, self-hatred, and inferiority, it also poses a threat to the larger community. This chapter explores the communal dimensions of nihilism, in particular, what is happening in the broader community that if unchanged raises the real specter of social disintegration and annihilation. Nihilism has given rise to a form of Social Darwinism, to increased racial prejudice and separatism, and a cold disregard for others. These three threaten the fabric of current communities and also threaten their future.

SOCIAL DARWINISM

Herbert Spencer developed the concept of Social Darwinism while witnessing the negative effects of the Industrial Revolution in England. In biological terms, Darwinism suggests the stronger and more adept species survive or evolve while the weaker eventually die out. This is commonly characterized as the process of natural selection. As a sociological doctrine, Social Darwinism suggests that the stronger members of society adapt, survive, thrive, and in some instances take advantage of the weaker and more vulnerable members. I believe this is happening today.

The conditions were ripe for Social Darwinism to flourish in black communities since the late seventies and early eighties, because of the inequitable distribution of wealth, the high rate of unemployment, and economic scarcity. In these conditions African Americans have a smaller piece of the economic pie to divide among themselves and there will be people with more than adequate means, people with adequate means, people with less than adequate means, and people with no means. These conditions are very Darwinistic and ripe for rivalry, exploitation, and violence.

The social conditions that necessitate such practices are a product of racism but the choice to adopt a survival of the fittest mindset is a product of nihilism. Black Social Darwinism manifests itself in the growing number of African Americans who exploit, oppress, and sometimes kill one another as a means of survival. And worse yet, too many have accepted the distorted beliefs about American success that is usually gained at the expense of the vulnerable. If some people believe there is only so much pie to go around then they will invariably fight over it. The problem today is that too many have adopted this line of thinking and living. There is evidence in the language and conversations in black communities that Social Darwinism is widespread.

"Player Haters"

One example that illustrates Darwinistic conditions is the preponderance of language about "player haters." Player hating is a colloquial expression in Hip Hop culture describing certain persons who are jealous of the material possessions someone has or the successes one enjoys. A "hater" expresses disdain for the person who has reached a level of achievement that they have not reached, often accusing the one experiencing success as thinking "they are better than others." As a result, these "haters" target people who have experienced some level of success with vitriol ranging from gossip and insults to more serious threats such as bullying and physical violence.

Both rappers and preachers talk about haters in songs and sermons. When these interpreters of black life talk about "haters" their listeners know exactly who they are referring to, because this is a popular expression. Interestingly both rappers and preachers encourage successful blacks not to be ashamed of what they have and what they have accomplished. The jealousy, resentment, and animosity they receive from "haters" should not prevent them from enjoying the fruit of their labors. More often than not, their advice is to ignore "haters" or worse yet to unapologetically flaunt their success. However, this only feeds the antagonism and rivalry between persons who may think the only way to succeed is by out-competing or exploiting someone else.

This language about "player haters" is instructive. "Haters" reflect conditions where there is scarcity and competition for limited resources. Because of this, success means getting a piece of the pie and dealing with jealousy, resentment, animosity, and sometimes violence from those left with the crumbs. It shows that part of the narrative of success in Black America is dealing with those who are not happy and possibly outright hostile about the success of others. But there is something deeply wrong with this narrative of success and the language of "haters" that fails to identify the larger conditions that breed jealousy. When African Americans accept such flawed logic our communities are left with antagonism and rivalry. In the end, antagonism and rivalry become the seeds of attitudes of neglect and disregard for less fortunate blacks.

"I'm Getting Mine!"

A second example of Darwinistic conditions is evident by the increased emphasis on individual success and prosperity in the past few decades. The focus is on the individual. The popular adage, "I'm getting mine," reflects the shift from communalism to individualism in the African American community. For example, three studies on various aspects of the contemporary black community suggest that younger blacks choose individualism over broader cultural concerns; that large segments of the black community have become obsessed with getting rich and career advancement; that some equate success with money; and that too many have adopted capitalistic or market values.[2] What these studies imply is that in varying ways, many in the black community are out to get their individual piece of the pie from gangsters, drug dealers, rappers, prosperity preachers, to young middle-class blacks, and not necessarily to help others in the black community.

For example, in the 1991 rap song "New Jack Hustler," Ice T personified drug lord Nino Brown, who is on top of his game as a drug dealer and businessmen. The lyrics are revealing. They reflect the nihilistic "get mine" mentality of black Social Darwinism. In the song Nino Brown's primary concern is money. He is cold and calculating. Personal profit, even at the expense of fellow blacks who suffer and die because of the drugs he sells, is the primary concern of Nino Brown. And while recognizing the problematic nature of the system (that he probably believes he cannot change), Brown drops out of school and works to become the top dog in the cold hard world of drugs. In the end, he chooses to profit at the expense of others. Hence, the stronger black survives and thrives but at the expense of vulnerable blacks.

Rappers like Ice T are not the only proponents of the "get mine" message that is inundating black communities; some religious leaders are following suit by proffering the

2. Kitwana, *The Hip-Hop Generation*, 6; Mitchem, *Name It Claim It*, 26–28; Harrison, *Righteous Riches*, 148–52.

prosperity gospel. Prosperity advocates such as Fred Price, Creflo Dollar, and Leroy Thompson teach their predominantly black congregations, among other things, that God wants them to drive the best cars, live in the best homes, and wear the best clothes because they are king's kids. It is not uncommon to hear a minister tell congregants that "they are going to get everything that God has for them," or worse yet that "money cometh," which is often understood in both monetary and individualistic terms. While it is important and well within the responsibilities of religious leaders to talk about issues such as finances, prosperity teachers tend to boast about their money in troubling ways that reflect the "get mine" nihilistic mindset.

> You can talk about me all you want while I'm driving by in my Rolls Royce that's paid for, and I got the pink slip on it. Talk all you want. Bad mouth all you want. Don't hurt me in the least. Doesn't bother me. It's a whole lot easier to be persecuted when I'm riding in my car and I got the pink slip than when it is I'm riding in a car and owe my soul to the company store.[3]

> I'm not preaching something I don't know about. I'm preaching "Money cometh" because it's working for me. Almost every four days, somebody gives me a check! My church is out of debt—way out of debt! And the same spirit that is upon me should be on you. One man from North Carolina recently gave me a check, crying, "'Money cometh' has changed my whole business! My wife and I are so blessed. Money cometh to us from everywhere! So here, Brother Thompson," and he handed me a check. He said, "I want you to have some money!" I said,

3. Price, "Ever Increasing Faith" program on TBN (March 29, 1992).

"Thank you." (Don't get the money and then
forget about the preacher).[4]

Pastors of African American congregations have middle-
class blacks as members but also have blacks who are lower
middle-class and working poor. These pastors receive monetary offerings from these people to support the church and
ministry efforts in the community. Yet prosperity pastors
such as Price and Thompson boast about driving expensive
cars and getting checks from people every four days as a
sign of God's blessings. Pouring through texts written by
advocates of the teaching, one cannot find any discussion
of the problematic nature of accumulating wealth through
monetary donations from people who, according to an ear-
lier study, are largely lagging behind European and Asian
Americans in every economic indicator—wealth, housing,
education, health care, etc. In the same way as Nino Brown,
profit by any means is the name of the game, even for some
pastors.

These African American prosperity teachers do not
understand prosperity in terms of affecting broader social
change that benefits others. Prosperity is not connected to
the health care crisis, educational reform, or remedying
poverty in most inner city and rural black communities.
The focus is on individual prosperity. By individually ap-
plying the principles of faith, such as sowing offerings to
churches, ministries, and pastors, and reaping spiritual
and financial blessings, one can prosper. Moreover, people
who do not prosper actually misrepresent God and are
ultimately at fault for not receiving what God has already
provided in the new covenant. This system where ministers
receive a steady flow of offerings from people of faith who
believe the monies are for the church and ministry gives

4. Thompson, *Money Cometh to the Body of Christ*, 12.

these ministers the proof needed to not only teach prosperity but also to use the monies to indict those without money as lacking faith. Prosperity teaching reflects a Darwinistic spirit as religious leaders feed on and exploit congregants.

These examples of "get mine" movements within black America signal the rise of Social Darwinism, and, resultantly have garnered the attention of prominent black intellectuals. Leaders offer sharp critiques of these movements because they reflect a much broader shift within the black community that undermines its ability to combat the social problems of the day. For example, Robert Franklin made an alarming charge when he said that the prosperity movement is "the single greatest threat to the historical legacy and core values of the contemporary Black church tradition."[5] This dire statement rests on his belief that this movement poses significant dangers for the future of the black church. In the early part of the twentieth century, it was not uncommon to see African American pastors driving through poor black communities in $100,000 vehicles, wearing designer clothes, and using large church facilities with extravagant décor. Though not uncommon to see, these practices have created controversy and stinging critiques like the one given by Franklin. Prosperity teachings subvert the principle of liberation and justice by their failure to address systemic and structural inequality. They prioritize individual attainment over communal and social responsibility. Milmon Harrison contends that many in African American prosperity churches do not seek to challenge or change the economic system but rather desire to prosper within the system.[6] In a real sense, certain aspects of prosperity teachings are nihilistic because of their focus on the individual and neglect of the broader society. Worse

5. Franklin, *Crisis in the Village*, 112.

6. Harrison, *Righteous Riches*, 149.

yet, prosperity teaching is nihilistic because one would expect religious institutions and its leaders to be concerned with God's mission in the world—i.e., society—instead of the individual's mission to succeed at the cost of others.

Black intellectuals have been correct in critiquing the increasing emphasis on individual success and how it undercuts the need to address broader systemic issues. But I think they miss the connection between the rising emphasis on individuality and nihilism. Racial oppression and discrimination have been so thoroughly internalized that blacks are increasingly opting for individual success. The claim, "I'm getting my piece of the pie," says something about the nihilistic mindset of some African Americans. The whole pie is out of the question and not in their purview and there is little concern for those who cannot eat any pie, or worse yet the plethora of problems in how the pie is divided in the first place. The attention is the individual quest for the little one can get. I argue that this practice relates to the concept of Social Darwinism that is applied to societies. But at its core, I believe that this move represents the acceptance of a more troubling belief that broader systemic and communal change is futile. Therefore, it is incumbent on thinkers and leaders in black communities to probe the link between individualism and nihilism because it threatens African Americans in the streets, in middle-class suburbs, and in the religious sector as well.

THE TURN AGAINST OTHERS

Nihilism also expresses itself in racial hostility that blacks hold toward whites and other ethnic minorities. Blacks not only turn on themselves but also turn on people who are not black. This is an additional dimension to the toll or racism that I have been discussing in this book. Racism not only affects African Americans economically and psychologically, but, when internalized, it manifests itself in a deep hatred for whites rooted in years of suffering and pain. Today, there are many African Americans who harbor deep resentment toward whites for both the history of slavery and segregation and the painful ways racism continues to affect their lives. In some cases, the resentment has turned into hatred. It is ironic that while some people claim that we live in a "post-racial" society that there are an increasing number of black people who hate white people. The result of this hatred is racial estrangement that further alienates marginalized blacks from relations that might bring help and hope. Girard identifies this aspect of mimesis as the "monstrous double." This idea is particularly germane to relations between blacks and non-blacks. He found that as "rivalry and combativeness between individuals (or groups) intensifies, characteristics that had previously distinguished them begin to dissolve." When this happens, "the antagonists effectively become doubles of each other."[7] Mimesis refers to imitation that occurs between groups in a given society. But what Girard points out is a particularly problematic element of it. In the case of a blood feud, he points out that it begins with a single act of murder that escalates across generations as distant relatives take vengeance on others for the singular act of murder. Mimesis then "becomes a chain reaction of vengeance in which human beings are constrained to the monotonous repetition of homicide. Vengeance turns them into doubles."[8] While each side has different reasons for violence both participate in it nonetheless becoming "monstrous doubles." In the case of racial antagonism in America, whites and blacks have been engaged in a social struggle for centuries. What Girard suggests is that over time whites and blacks so mir-

7. Fleming, *Rene Girard*, 42.
8. Ibid., 45 (quoting Girard).

ror one another that eventually they become doubles who both are given over to the power of racial animosity. In the end blacks, who were formerly victims of racial violence, sometimes participate in and or mirror the very evil they sought to resist.

Girard's concept of the monstrous double provides understanding into the prejudicial attitudes and behaviors of blacks against other racial ethnic groups. Blacks who have been stereotyped, classified, categorized, and excluded because of racist beliefs and values are now doing these same things to people of other ethnic groups. In my work as a religious leader, I have encountered increasing instances of blacks participating in bias and racist behavior against European, Asian, and Hispanic American people. I was particularly surprised and disappointed to find that religious people were, in some instances, some of the most prejudiced persons I have encountered. Some of these persons are not shy in expressing their disdain for people of other ethnicities, in making pejorative statements about the bodily features of non-blacks, and in making comparisons that subtly imply that other ethnicities are inferior to them. Worse yet, there was little in their religious tradition that they drew on to challenge such prejudicial and racist statements, beliefs, and practices. I have sat through too many painful conversations with blacks who spew out racist venom toward people who are not black. These racist statements left me extremely disappointed and reflect deep-seated prejudices and racial hostility toward people of other ethnicities. The irony of this is that blacks have begun to do to others the very things done to them. African Americans who are prejudiced and exude racial animosity toward others seem to go against their history of struggle and freedom. When considering that few ethnic groups understand the pain of racism better than African Americans, it is hard to reconcile the hostility that is gaining a foothold in black communities.

The nihilistic turn against others not only expresses itself in racial hostility but also in practices of excluding non-blacks from familial relationships and institutions. Nihilism has a communal expression of exclusion that concretizes racial estrangement and alienation in American communities. A few years ago I met a Mexican American minister who worked with Baptist congregations across the state, establishing Hispanic ministries that provide an array of spiritual and social services. He was very passionate about his work and the importance of enlisting more partners in churches to serve this growing segment of the community. I couldn't wait to hear how many African American congregations were involved in this vital ministry. I was excited as I considered some of the struggles the black and Hispanic communities have endured in America and how partnerships can strengthen justice initiatives in poor communities. I saw this as a great opportunity for the church to exercise leadership and vision in the broader community. But the minister told me that he could not find one African American Baptist congregation willing to have a Hispanic ministry in its church. Only two congregations entertained the possibility, but once the action was formally voted on it did not pass. Even though the minister did not ask every pastor in the state, he had solicited enough congregations to get the impression that black churches were not interested in ministering to the Hispanic community. On the few occasions I have had the opportunity to share this story with African American churches some expressed their dismay that no church was willing to open its doors to the Hispanic community. However, there were voices in the churches that said, "The church is the only thing we have left and if we allow others to come in they will take over" or "They need to have their own churches because we can't understand them." For them, these reasons justified the failure to be hospitable to people in need, particularly to people who are different. This is one example, among many others, I could share about the kind of bias and exclusion present in some parts of African American communities.

What appears to be a defense mechanism or a survivalist impulse, closing oneself off from others, actually further undermines a holistic sense of self and community. People who internalize racial oppression turn against others, missing the fact that beyond our ethnic differences, we are all a part of the human family. Opportunities to build stronger communities are also missed. This form of nihilism is counterproductive because it cuts marginalized persons off from relationships and partnerships that can bring healing and revitalization to black communities. People who are vulnerable and need support will not benefit from pushing others away, no matter how they rationalize it. Exclusion exacerbates the plight of the African American community.

For religious leaders like Reginald Davis, to say that the African American community is in trouble is an understatement because nihilism threatens to tear the already weakened fabric of black communities even more. The emergence of Social Darwinism, racial hostility, and exclusion leaves the black community exploited and isolated. In a real sense, the dual turn—blacks turning on blacks and blacks turning on non-blacks—can lead to social annihilation. Internalized despair, self-hatred, and inferiority manifest through both self-destructive and self-defeating lifestyles, as well as through communal practices of exploitation and exclusion. Nihilistic blacks have adopted the flawed racialized imagination of the dominant culture. In doing this, they accept that the social world of America is fundamentally racialized, so that persons should be categorized and stereotyped on the basis of race. This belief is what race theorists call the social construction of race. Furthermore, this way of viewing the world governs all social relations. In other words, blacks participate in racial formation on both the personal and institutional levels, building communities and identities to perpetuate racial hostility. Worse yet, because the social order is thoroughly racialized, nihilistic blacks adopt the racist ethical framework where fear, hatred, deception, exploitation, and violence are acceptable practices. But accepting the social construction of race and forming blacks in the ways of racialization has detrimental effects on their ability to combat the external and internal dimensions of racial evil. Nihilistic blacks participate in the evil they sought to combat and suffer its devastating consequences. After the stronger members of the black community finish feeding on its weaker members while becoming increasingly hostile toward non-blacks, our communities could be socially decimated or severely impaired. In the end, nihilism poses a formidable threat.

BLACKS WHO DON'T GIVE A FUCK

To internalize racism is to accept racist beliefs and stereotypes about blacks and non-blacks, to accept the normative presence of racism in America, to believe that racist categories are binding on all relations between blacks and non-blacks, and worse yet, to give in to and participate in self-hatred, exploitation, and violence as counterproductive responses to the legitimate anger one feels because of the experience of racism. The undercurrent of unresolved anger fuels nihilism. On a deeper level, nihilism produces a defiant attitude in some blacks similar to Kitwana's description of movie portrayals of urban youth as the ones who don't "give a fuck." This is an abrasive term but one that very much resonates with a nihilistic culture. This description is referring to a fundamental disregard for others and for change. I have seen this attitude among blacks who don't care how bad things get in their lives and communities. It is almost as if a wall is constructed to keep everyone out. In the end, "not giving a fuck" makes it incredibly difficult to get help for yourself and to work for change in black communities. This pervasive lack of concern is the final vestige of a nihilism that can potentially decimate black communities. However, in contrast to Kitwana's description, black youth are not the only ones who don't give a fuck.

Rappers have been giving voice to the nihilism in their respective communities for decades. Some describe their communities as a living hell, as places of grinding poverty, injustice, hopelessness, hatred, and violence. Rap songs such as Eric B and Rakim's "I Ain't No Joke," Talib Kweli's "Give 'Em Hell," Eminem's "Welcome to Hell," and Raekwon's debut single "Heaven and Hell" are examples of this pervasive belief. In rap music, hell is an apropos image and description of the harsh realities rappers experience. It is possible that there is no better evidence of nihilism than oppressed persons who describe their life in such dark and stark terms as "welcome to hell" or "take a walk through hell."

These poets of culture are bold in their critique of the hypocrisy of America and defiant in their refusal to assimilate into an unjust mainstream. Instead they brandish a "fuck you" mentality and find meaning and joy in sexual pleasure, gang violence, and different forms of community and family. Rappers and African Americans in inner cities aren't the only ones experiencing nihilism. Some upper middle-class African Americans and pastors of prosperity churches are nihilistic as well. There is a blindness and deafness to the plight of poor blacks by upper middle-class blacks that is nihilistic. While their language is more refined than rappers, the basic "fuck you, that's not my problem" message still remains. For two and a half decades, black prosperity preachers peddled a materialistic gospel that excited impoverished blacks with the promise of riches that only the preachers enjoyed. Under the garb of religion and the language of blessings, prosperity preachers said, "Fuck you" to the larger issues of economic injustice and a capitalistic system that leaves most blacks unemployed and impoverished. "Get your individual blessing because we don't care about justice in the world" is just as nihilistic as drug dealers making profit off the drugs killing people in his or her own community. In the end, the challenge of nihilism, at its core, is to find a way to construct identities, communities, and a vision of change among those who don't care, or at least say they don't care, if things improve. If such a vision is not found, communities may continue to languish.

Nihilism must be confronted head-on by creative, bold, and courageous leaders. In order to address the effects of internalized racial oppression (nihilism), the social effects and psychological or spiritual effects must be addressed. Leaders in the African American community must confront nihilism on both fronts. We must continue to attend to pressing social issues such as education, health care, home ownership, the prison industrial complex, unemployment, wealth disparities, voter registration, etc. These issues speak to the painful realities of inequity that still persist and the devastating numbers of poor blacks in America. But leaders must also attend to the hopelessness, self-hatred, and inferiority that manifest itself through irresponsible, destructive, and self-defeating lifestyles adopted by an increasing number of African Americans. The "fuck it" mentality of too many blacks only insures our continued suffering as victims of racism, instead of resisting racism and persisting in building strong communities and persons with healthy identities.

Four

Nihilism and the Crisis of Black Religion

WITH HER VOICE TREMBLING and tears in her eyes, she asked me, "If God can't do this one thing for me then what is all this for? Why am I doing this?" I will never forget that conversation. She had a particular need in mind that she prayed and hoped God would meet. But for me, I knew this conversation represented so much more. This unmet need represented a crisis of faith because her church teaches that a believer can confess and stand in faith for a blessing and God would answer. She has been waiting for years but God has not answered yet. Beyond the persistence of her confession and continued sacrificial service to that church, her tears and words betray deeper doubts and fears. These doubts and fears are centered on the reality of her situation that looks like it is not going to change in spite of the sincerity of her faith. So she asks why she is doing this if God can't grant her this one thing. As a biblical and religious scholar, I wanted to say, "That is a good question. Maybe we need to talk about your church's understanding of God." But in the moment, all I could do was gently brace her for the prospect that this desire may not be answered but that doesn't mean her faith is in vain. I can't help but wonder if she will abandon religion altogether or leave the church if it fails to meet her deepest need, or will she continue to go to church and worship with deep fears and insecurities about the efficacy of faith in God in addressing the unique needs of blacks in America?

The tears in her eyes and desperation in her voice is a part of the story of black nihilism. Her disappointment and pain were real. The prospects that her religion could not change her condition had a crushing effect on her. From the desperation in her voice, I could tell that her pastor and other preachers she has heard had not explored the question of meaning for those left out and left behind in the "get mine" culture in some churches. From that day on, I have given considerable thought to this conversation and others like it I have had with black Christians who are wrestling with deep fears and questions that they cannot give voice to in their congregations. They attend churches with different beliefs and worship practices, yet their struggles to make sense of the perplexities they face are similar. I began to see how the inability of some religious institutions and beliefs to address existing existential and social conditions is an important factor in the frustration, despair, apathy, resentment, and anger that some blacks struggle with today. And the root of these feelings is a gnawing fear that God and religious devotion may not be able to change the dire social conditions that they face, or address the crisis of meaninglessness and hopelessness eating away at the black spirits. So I conclude this study of nihilism in black America with a focus on the frustrations and anxieties that have emerged when religion, for whatever reason, fails to meet black people's deepest needs or change conditions that rob them of joy, love, and hope. I believe this is an early sign of a religious crisis connected to nihilism affecting churches, synagogues, mosques, and other religious centers.

THE CRISIS OF MEANING

In order to understand the religious dimensions of black nihilism, I turn to two eighteenth-century figures not commonly believed to help us explore the black religious experience, Friedrich Nietzsche and Karl Marx, and to an often quoted and noted contemporary black historian, Albert Raboteau. Their work helps me to understand the fear, frustration, hurt, and extreme disappointment prevalent in parts of the black community. Black nihilism resembles the nihilism that affected Europeans in the eighteenth century and today, though nascent, is affecting a growing number of blacks who attend Christian churches. Nihilism's rise in Europe was not just a rejection of Christian beliefs and values, but a growing recognition of the inadequacy of these beliefs to address the pressing existential questions of the day. Nietzsche argued that nihilism is the result of two realizations and one conclusion. First, he points to the discouragement that emerges "when we have sought a meaning in all events that is not there." Second, he mentions the exacerbation that results "when one has posited a totality, a systemization . . . but behold there is no such universal." Nietzsche is speaking about the realization that there is no grand unity or order in life. These dual points lead to a conclusion. He says a person passes "sentence on this whole world of becoming as a deception and to invent the world beyond it, a true world."[1] Nietzsche identifies nihilism as ultimately a crisis of meaning and hope intricately tied to meaninglessness in the world. When the world or society does not make

---

1. Nietzsche, *The Will to Power*, 12–13.

sense, people are left with nihilism or nothing. Out of the nothingness of life, one turns to something for meaning. Nietzsche makes a lot of sense for the experience of black people in America. The meaninglessness of being a slave, or living during segregation, or the plethora of ways blacks suffer today in prisons or in unemployment lines or being harassed by white police officers, or in communities with dilapidated houses and abandoned factories, causes us to search for meaning.

Karl Marx is an important figure because of the way he illumines why people, particularly marginalized people, turn to religion. In other words, Marx helps us to identify the function of religion in a society. In America, dire social conditions in predominantly black communities affect why and how African Americans turn to religion. Because their conditions and needs are unique, the character of black religion will be unique. This is why black religion can be described as the opiate of the oppressed. Marx developed the phrase "religion is the opiate of the masses" in the introduction of his work *Contribution to Critique of Hegel's Philosophy of Right,* written in 1843. He said, "Religious suffering is at the same time an expression of real suffering and a protest against real suffering. Religion is the sigh of the oppressed creature, the sentiment of a heartless world, and the soul of soulless conditions. It is the opium of the people."[2] Opiates are often associated with pain relief or pleasure. One would think of religious opium as that which helps people deal with pain in life and to feel better or hopeful about life. But for Marx, religion is the opium that provides illusory beliefs that enable the disenfranchised to accept an unjust social order, many times by focusing on the afterlife or heaven. Marx goes on to call for the aboli-

2. Marx, *Contribution to Critique of Hegel's Philosophy of Right,* 131.

tion of religion, which he understood as a product of the human imagination. However, to accomplish this requires one to address the suffering that pushes one to the illusion of religion.

What is helpful about his analysis is the link between dire social conditions that produce suffering and the turn to religion. I appropriate this aspect of Marx's thought on religion without accepting his premise that religion and God are projections of the human imagination and desire for a better world, which I find highly problematic. People turn to religion because they are suffering and searching for meaning. Historically, this has been one of the functions of black religion. While this is not the only reason African Americans turn to religion, it is a helpful way to understand the unique ways social conditions, and the needs created by such conditions, influence the turn to religion. This has been true from the days of slavery, Jim Crow segregation, the Civil Rights movement, and today as African Americans confront the nihilistic crisis.

UNANSWERED QUESTIONS AND LINGERING DOUBTS IN CHURCHES

If suffering is an important factor in the turn to religion, then two important functions of religion are to give meaning both to those who suffer and the conditions that cause suffering. Suffering and meaninglessness must command the attention and intellectual energies of religious leaders like pastors. Yet today some leaders are unaware of widespread suffering in black communities, social conditions that guarantee suffering continues, and the crisis of meaninglessness that this causes. Nihilism is lurking in their pews and some pastors are oblivious to this. For too many black pastors, smiling faces, amens, and a few hallelujah shouts are all the proof they need that people are fine. If they would spend enough time with people in more personal settings and give people space to share their joys and concerns, they would be surprised at the deep angst that is hidden behind smiles and the popular religious jargon. Worse yet, some pastors may be unable to address this angst with much of the shallow idealism that characterizes their preaching and teaching. "God will make a way somehow," "I got a feeling everything is gonna be all right," "we're going to the next level," and "somebody is gonna get a blessing" are popular phrases in black churches, but they betray a shallow theology that God is going to work things out for faithful black Christians while ignoring deeper questions about the overall social conditions of blacks and the inequities that continue to destroy our communities and rob many of hope and opportunity to thrive. The question the woman at the beginning of this chapter asked—"If God can't do this one thing then what is all this for?"—is tacit proof of the inadequacy of theological beliefs in some black churches to speak to these issues. Obviously things have not worked out for her and she has not received her blessing, and she wants to know why this has to be. It has been quite a few years and she has yet to receive an answer.

But maybe there are reasons black pastors and teachers don't touch these issues—why things are the way they are for blacks. Deep questions that arise from conditions that make black suffering and inequity permanent touch on a very old and deep nerve. In fact, I would describe this as one of the ghosts that haunt black spirits and is often ignored because of where the questions may lead. Under the fervor and frenzy of black religious worship are deep questions and fears. If African Americans cannot rely on God then who or what can they rely on? Does God and religion make life better for blacks?

Doubts, fears, and questioning the effectiveness of religious devotion for giving meaning, hope and improvement to their plight is not new for African Americans. They have wrestled with deep religious questions for centuries, especially attempting to draw on religion to give meaning to the crisis of slavery and segregation. However, as blacks wrestled with religious questions oftentimes that rose because of intense suffering, not all of them believed that religion provided the meaning and hope they were looking for. Some were deeply religious persons yet came to moments of crisis when religion was no longer able to help them make sense of the senselessness of being a slave or always a second-class citizen. As a result, blacks switched religions and sometimes turned away from religion altogether.

Turning away from religion contradicts the popular religious narrative of blacks because it is commonly believed they embraced Christian belief in spite of the oppressive and dehumanizing conditions of slavery and segregation, without giving due attention to the difficult questions these conditions raised for them. In fact, one of the largely ignored facts of African American history was the number of enslaved Africans who rejected Christianity. Why did they reject Christianity? First, they were introduced to Christianity under a system of institutionalized slavery supported by persons in the government and the church who professed to be Christians. Second, for those who became Christians, they were forced to share the faith of their oppressors, which was difficult for some to justify. It was challenging to conceive of a religion that both supported their dehumanization as slaves and yet gave meaning to them as God's people. And third, the reality that, in spite of their religious status, their condition would not dramatically improve was troublesome. They could be saved from their sins and called children of God, but at day's end they were still slaves. These and other reasons posed formidable obstacles to their faith. For example, Daniel Alexander Payne observed the struggle with Christian religion among enslaved Africans in the nineteenth century. He states,

> They hear their masters professing Christianity; they see their masters preaching the gospel; they hear these masters praying in their families, and they know that oppression and slavery are inconsistent with the Christian religion; therefore they scoff at religion itself—mock their masters and distrust both the goodness and justice of God. Yes, I have known even to question his existence. I speak not what others have told me, but of what I have both seen and heard from the slaves themselves.[3]

Bishop Payne observed slaves who could not become a Christian because it did not make sense to them, it did not give them meaning and hope and would not dramatically change their condition.

For enslaved Africans, one of the primary functions of Christianity was to give meaning to what was, at the time, a permanent social condition, and to explore what it meant to have hope. Religion was very helpful for some and not as helpful to others. In an essay on religious life in the slave community, Albert Raboteau describes an array of responses to the dilemmas of slavery. He discusses both the large number of enslaved Africans who accepted various forms of Christianity, but also those who rejected it. On Sunday mornings, there were many enslaved Africans that attended worship. Preachers were licensed by the church and hired by the master to instruct the slaves. Often in addition to worship sanctioned by the master, enslaved Africans would

3. Douglas Strange, "Document: Bishop Alexander Payne's Protestation of American Slavery," quoted in Albert Raboteau, *Slave Religion*, 313.

conduct their own prayer meetings characterized by intense and emotionally charged worship. On the other hand, there were "nonreligious slaves (who) spent Sunday's hunting, fishing, marble shooting, storytelling, or simply resting when allowed."[4] Raboteau even intimated that nonreligious blacks resented being forced to attend church. What partly influenced the rejection of the Christian religion was their core perception of Christianity as "white's man religion" used to justify oppression. His brief discussion of the unbelief that permeated the slave community was provided to "temper generalizations about the piety of all slaves."[5]

This is a helpful way to understand the variety of ways blacks turned away from or to religion to give meaning and hope to their condition. It also sheds some light on the disappointment that woman discussed at the beginning of this chapter was feeling. Her pain is not new. It is a core part of the black religious struggle for meaning and hope amidst difficult conditions that do not appear to be changing. While our ancestors struggled with slavery and segregation, blacks today confront the crisis of nihilism and its effect on the religion of African Americans. The work of Nietzsche, Marx, and Raboteau provide a lens on what is happening with the black church today. The woman's pain is a microcosm of a religious problem for the black church. Unlike her, not all blacks are going to stay in churches or accept a religion that fails to address the social crisis of the day. They will not turn their gaze to heaven or a spiritual kingdom that provides supposed "blessings" to the faithful. There are, already, an increasing number who are turning away from church.

4. Raboteau, *Slave Religion*, 225.
5. Ibid., 314.

THE REVERSAL OF THE HISTORIC TURN TO RELIGION

For centuries, many African Americans have turned to religion to find comfort, meaning, and hope amid the difficulties and paradoxes they encountered. Black congregations have provided spaces where blacks feel safe and free to express their joys and the frustrations of being slaves or living in a segregated society. In these spaces, the spiritual, communal, and ideological resources of religion were drawn on to give meaning and hope to the meaninglessness and hopelessness of a marginalized existence. Religion, especially the black church, has been an integral part of the black community's ability to withstand racism and thrive as a people. Black churches have sought to meet the needs of black people, providing not just space to worship and pray but also being instrumental in the development of black institutions such as mutual aid societies, schools, banks, insurance companies, and even fraternities and sororities.

Because of the expansive influence and reach of the black church, it has historically held a central place in the black community. If you drive through an African American community, you will see churches on almost every corner. And black people regularly attend these churches. In the late part of the twentieth century, one study of the black church found that 78 percent of the black population claimed church membership and attended church once in the last six months, while 44 percent of blacks attended church on a weekly basis. Blacks also have the highest rates of being super-churched, meaning they attend church more than once a week.[6] Religious devotion is a hallmark of the black community.

6. Lincoln and Mamiya, *The Black Church in the African American Experience*, 382.

For the most part, the turn to religion was understood as a turn to something that could make things better. However, the historic turn to religion is changing. There are an increasing number of blacks who are now turning away from religious institutions like churches. The signs are everywhere of a growing disconnect with the church and a belief that the church is unable and sometimes unwilling to address the pressing issues of blacks. For example, John W. Fountain, a *Washington Post* journalist, writing for the *Courier Journal,* penned an article exploring his disconnect with the contemporary black church as a microcosm of the tens of thousands of black men who no longer attend black churches.[7] Fountain expresses his dismay at the disinterest black churches have in reaching black men and his disdain for the materialism of black clergy who exploit poor congregants. He is also very critical of the ways black denominations and churches do not use the money they collect to build homes for the elderly, recreation centers, and new business developments. Further evidence of this change can be found by Eddie Glaude's article two years ago entitled, "The Black Church is Dead." He published the article in the *Huffington Post* and created a major debate about the importance of the Black Church. Glaude contends that while religion is important to African Americans, the idea that the black church is central to the religious lives of blacks has long been abandoned. He says blacks no longer need the black church to be religious. Scores of pastors and church leaders across the nation took issue with Glaude's claim that the black church is dead. They claimed that the black church is as viable today as it has ever been to the religious lives of black people. However, the misleading title of his essay and the ensuing debate over the supposed "death" of

7. John W. Fountain, "I still love God but I've lost faith in the Black Church," *The Courier Journal* (date unknown): H1, H5.

the black church has caused people to miss the core issue Glaude sought to raise, which is the decentralization of the black church in the African American community. He was identifying what is clear in black communities across the country, that there has been and continues to be a gradual exodus from the black church. There are growing number of African Americans who choose to practice their faith outside the bounds of the black church, blacks who choose to practice non-Christian religions and blacks who reject any religion. This does not even include the high number of African Americans whose attendance and participation in church is sporadic or marginal at best. One could say that in some respects the black church as a central institution that blacks primarily turn to is dead. That is, however, not to say that black churches do not exist or are no longer important, which is not true.

Today, African American churches are also being challenged as irrelevant institutions that do not significantly help black communities. In *The Black Church: Relevant or Irrelevant in the 21st Century*, Reginald Davis grapples with the growing irrelevance of black churches. For him, the question of relevance is intricately tied to whether the black church will address the continuing suffering of black communities. Black Americans rank at the top in crime, murders, drug abuse, unemployment, incarceration, poverty, education, education deficiencies, and HIV/AIDS. Yet, so many in black churches are not addressing these issues in public venues and are not involved in making substantive changes in these trends. Davis views the black church as a sleeping giant amidst a people in crisis, and contends that the people in most black churches are "addicted to religiosity instead of liberation" and that the black church "spends more time, energy, and resources on non-liberating activities like church programs, annual days, conferences, and conventions than on liberating the community from economic social, and political oppression."[8] African American congregations are being challenged to do more than provide spaces for religious activities like worship, prayer, and preaching. They are expected to affect change in communities in decline.

What is happening to religious institutions like black churches and why is it that they are unable to meet people's needs? Jawanza Kunjufu's typologies of the black church are a helpful beginning point. He argues that there are three types of black churches: entertainment churches, containment churches, and liberation churches.[9] His typologies are illustrative of a belief that some black churches are preoccupied with entertainment or have congregants so busy with church services and activities that they do not serve the larger community. Two of the three models were deemed unhelpful to the black community and Kunjufu gives evidence that the dominant culture of black churches privilege the entertainment-containment model, which he sought to challenge. Furthermore, his typology suggests that the reason black churches are not meeting needs, mentioned by Davis and others, is that they are more interested in offering people entertainment or consolation. In fact, I believe that the reason black churches are so interested in making people feel good is because of the ways nihilistic conditions are robbing them of life.

THE TURN TO FEEL-GOOD RELIGION

Today black churches and pastors are in the business of making blacks feel better. They are increasingly using the

8. Davis, *The Black Church*, 35–36.

9. Kunjufu, *Adam Where Art Thou*, 23–24.

resources of religion, such as worship and preaching, to accomplish this task. The truth is some black people come to church to be entertained and want a religion that makes them feel good. It is common to hear people in black churches pray "don't let us leave the same way we came." Beneath the language of this prayer is evidence of a belief that not only can worship transform a person but, if done in the right spirit, it can even make a person feel better. Black people come to church with an expectation of feeling better. So the religious encounter is approached with this subtle expectation. What we've seen in the past few decades is a culture that accommodates the need and desire to feel better. Because people turn to church to feel better, leaders in churches respond accordingly but do so without understanding the suffering, using Marx's term, and the undercurrent of nihilism that drives some people to church.

For example, singing in African American churches has undergone changes during the last two decades, and these changes are a signal of the nihilistic wound that seeks salve in worship. Martha Simmons's study of trends in the black church listed praise teams as a major trend. She says praise teams give preliminary evidence of a shift away from congregational singing.[10] Simmons identifies a fundamental shift in the culture of many African American churches away from a participatory form of worship to a spectacular form of worship. Congregants no longer sing together but are led in worship by a praise team. Praise teams have become popular in black churches for well over a decade. But what has happened as a result of praise teams is a more passive and spectacular form of worship, where blacks sit and watch people sing and sometimes even dance. There is considerable tension in black congregations regarding praise teams who have to wake up, pump up, or excite the people

10. Simmons, "Trends in the African American Church," 14.

to respond to God. Many pastors and praise leaders remind congregants that there was a time when black people did not have to be pumped up or excited to praise God. This little tension is a sign of a passiveness and lethargy already present in black churches. The tendency to spectate has become a dominant way of worship and a signal of a need to be ministered to or made to feel better. For some reason, black people come to church but don't feel like standing, clapping, and or raising their hands to God.

Black preaching has an integral role in feel-good religion. Two things are clear about some forms of contemporary black preaching. The first is that black sermons are increasingly addressing the existential crisis of black social conditions. Yet they are doing this by focusing on individuals persons. Many sermons in black churches, especially those of pastors who televise their worship services, are existential sermons that seek to speak a life-giving word to people's circumstances. Sermons explore themes such as success and defeat, jealousy, hope, breakthrough, new beginnings, second chances, the family, financial prosperity, faith, loss, and victory. These sermons convince blacks that God is concerned about them and if they believe in God's plan and live faithfully, they will overcome insurmountable obstacles like those biblical heroes faced in their lives. Existential preaching has become a dominant focus in many black congregations while doctrinal preaching and preaching on social issues, which require giving attention to one's social and historical context and structural issues, is given an inadequate amount of attention. Congregants pour into black churches to hear a sermon tailored to their existential dilemmas and judge the value of a sermon on the basis of whether it speaks to their condition.

The second point is that these sermons often reflect an otherworldly or heavenly cosmology, talking about Satan, demons, curses, the spirit world, and spiritual kingdoms. Because of this otherworldly or heavenly focus, often these sermons neglect or completely ignore political, social, and economic issues of this world. The knowledge and language of large segments of black Christianity are very much otherworldly and heavenly. So if black persons who go to church ask why they are poor, they are likely to hear their pastor tell them it is because of the devil or a demonic curse that can be broken over their lives with a special prayer or confession or offering. There is very little talk about the economic benefit whites received from centuries of slavery, the ways blacks were systematically exploited working for centuries without proper remuneration, or how discrimination continues to impact the ability of some blacks to thrive. So over time, after much prayer, and thousands of dollars of offerings given to churches and preachers, there are still a large number of black Christians who are just as poor now as they have ever been. And worse yet, their focus is on spiritual and unseen forces instead of those wielded in the material world in which they live, which is a major factor as to why there are so many poor blacks.

The real difficulty with the kind of preaching that characterizes feel-good religion is that it does not give meaning to the realities and powers that truly rob black people of joy, peace, and love. Again, this is why the lady in the introduction was so afraid. She was beginning to see the futility of a religion that does not really address the crisis of her life. Her story resembles the story of many in churches with feel-good religion. There is singing and a sincere attempt to give meaning to difficult life issues, but the individual focus and failure to address social and historical backdrop against which to cast black life, leaves too many black Christians with just warm feelings, unanswered questions, and a faith that God is the one to fix all this. In this sense, feel-good religion functions as an effective opiate. Feel-good religion may be popular and helpful in ameliorating temporal feelings of despair and sadness but it fails to address the forces responsible for black nihilism.

FROM BLACK CHURCH TO RELIGION

Instead of black people turning to church as a reliable source of inspiration, meaning and hope, there are a growing number of blacks who are very critical of the black church and resultantly leaving congregations. What is happening in African American churches is a microcosm of larger concerns about the efficacy and value of religion for the black community. For some, the black church has become a space that merely entertains black people and it repeatedly fails to draw on the resources of religion to address the social problems that are hurting the black community. Some even challenge some preachers for exploiting the very people they are called to serve. Are these critiques a sign that the end of religion is at hand?

It is apparent that people are critical of the black church because they have expectations of what it is able to do for the black community beyond providing space for religious activities. Yet what is not clear is whether or not they expect the black church to continue to be the central institution of the community, when black people have already begun decentralizing it as such. African Americans do not always look to the church as the central institution or hope of the community. These critiques are instructive. They demonstrate the pervasive belief in black America that religion is either the answer or a major source of hope for African Americans. And these beliefs inform the expectations that even black scholars have of African American congregations and pastors.

Like the woman who was taught to believe that faith in God was the answer to whatever she thought she needed, even our scholars look to rightly practiced religion as the answer for what ails black Americans. Maybe they believe that "if the church did its job, things would be better." I cannot help but to wonder if part of some of the critiques against the black church is an underlying belief that the religion of the black church can save the black community from the nihilism that centuries of racism produces. I wonder, is it possible for the black church to be the savior of the black community with such limited financial and human capital at its disposal? I have some doubts. Certainly it is reasonable to expect the black church to do its share in the community. But it is unreasonable to expect the church to do everything because it is impractical to expect a single institution to meet so many needs, and it is philosophically dangerous to centralize an imperfect human institution as the source of hope for oppressed communities.

Carter Woodson stated, "The Negro church, in the absence of other agencies . . . has had to do more than its duty in taking care of the general interests of the race."[11] Because of this, he refers to the black church as the all comprehending institution. What this means is that the black church serves as a resource in all matters religious, social, political, and economic. Black churches function as institutions that serve their communities in ways qualitatively different than white churches. Black churches, as surrogate institutions, are looked to and expected to meet the needs of black people and the black community. But the reality is that there is always more need than resources available.

From my twenty years of experience as a pastor and seven years a theological educator, I can attest to the

11. Woodson, "The Negro Church, an All Comprehending Institution," 7.

demand the black community puts upon the church. Our churches provide spiritual and material food, money to pay past due light bills and late rent, among other things. When someone does not have enough money to meet basic needs, they look to the church for benevolence. I remember the increasing number of people calling the church I pastored in 2008 after the economic collapse. There was considerable need in the community and we did not have enough financial resources to meet them. This put an incredible amount of pressure on the leadership to manage limited resources and also deal with the grief and guilt for turning people away.

Another example of the lack of resources to meet so much need is the relatively small number of black pastors with theological training. One study of the contemporary black church found that approximately 20 to 30 percent of ministers in black churches are seminary trained and that ministry is the only class of black professionals where the majority of practitioners do not have graduate training.[12] That means that anywhere between 70 to 80 percent of ministers leading black churches are not trained in biblical languages, Christian history and theology, ethics, practical theology, and church administration. While there is still a debate about the importance of theological education in black churches, it is reasonable to conclude that such a high number of untrained clergy makes it difficult for pastors to adequately respond to the challenges of ministry and the theological questions blacks have about the world in which they live. The shallow idealism of contemporary black preaching is related to the high number of black clergy who do not have the training to develop theologies that speak to the deep issues and needs of blacks. They are attempting to be faithful to the eternal souls of blacks while neglect-

---

12. Mamiya, "River of Struggle, River of Freedom," 4.

ing the social forces destroying their souls in the first place. And too many pastors don't know where to begin or how to begin to take up this challenge.

Black congregations and their leaders serve as surrogates in a plethora of ways. While this is a distinguishing feature and strength of the historic black church, we must not overlook the toll this has taken on institutions and leaders with a limited amount of resources, and how they have sought to balance meeting so many varied needs. In the same way that we valorize blacks as overcoming against all odds, we tend to valorize the black church as if serving marginalized people for centuries does not weaken or lessen its effectiveness over time. The truth is, black churches are not all comprehending institutions and cannot meet all the needs of blacks. A critical component of the turn away from the church and other religious institutions is the inevitable nature of it when so much demand is placed upon one institution. While religion is a vast resource, religious institutions, leaders, and the resources required to meet material needs have definite limits. But this does not mean there is no hope for black America. In fact, adjusting our expectations of religious instituions is exactly what needs to happen if black America is going to escape the abyss of nihilism and find hope.

Black America needs more than preachers "with a word from God" and a good worship service every week to help our communities. Churches and pastors need strategic partnerships with organizations and agencies in the broader community. Black America needs congregational ministers like bishops and pastors, and also "community ministers" like teachers, lawmakers, activists, social workers, counselors, philosophers, law enforcement officials, businessmen and women, construction workers, and health care and other professionals in order to address the crisis of nihilism. Past are the days of valorizing the black church as the singular entity of hope for black America. God has always been and will always be bigger than the institutional church, and maybe our future hope resides in widening our gaze to discern God in other places. In the end this can lessen the weight put upon churches and give churches space to take up the task of giving meaning to suffering and hopelessness in black communities. This task will require denominations and churches to make substantive changes in how it does business in black communities and will require better educated clergy who can help black Americans make sense of the senselessness of nihilism.

The woman I have mentioned throughout this chapter asked "if God can't do this one thing for me then what is all this for? Why am I doing this?" Her question is not a reflection of a nascent form of atheism but rather a level of questioning that is necessary for black Christians of all denominational traditions. It is time to rethink how black religion serves and push the boundaries of our thinking beyond shallow anecdotes and beliefs that are disconnected from the spiritual and social forces affecting the lives of all people. The woman's question is a helpful first step toward rejecting any form of feel-good religion. And her question is representative of a deeper search for meaning and care for life that can revitalize faith and churches. As the nihilistic crisis reaches its climax and hopefully dissipates, persons with deep religious beliefs and values must push for deeper expressions that give meaning and hope to a community wracked by centuries of racial oppression and despair. In the end, black nihilism's lasting legacy may be the renewal of faith.

Bibliography

Asante, Molefi Kete. *An Afrocentric Manifesto*. Cambridge, UK: Polity, 2007.

Ashby, Homer. *Our Home Is Over Jordan: A Black Pastoral Theology*. St. Louis: Chalice, 2003.

Ashimolo, Matthew. *What Is Wrong With Being Black?* Shippensburg, PA: Destiny Image, 2007.

Bailey, Randall C., ed. *The Recovery of Black Presence*. Nashville: Abingdon, 1995.

Bell, Derrick. *Faces at the Bottom of the Well: The Permanence of Racism*. New York: Basic, 1992.

Bennett, William J., John J. Dilulio, Jr., and John P. Walters. *Body Count: Moral Poverty and How to Win America's War Against Crime and Drugs*. New York: Simon and Schuster, 1996.

Berlin, Ira, et al. *Remembering Slavery: African Americans Talk About Their Experiences of Slavery and Emancipation*. New York: The New Press, 1998.

Breasted, James Henry. *Ancient Times: A History of the Early World*, 2nd ed., revised and largely rewritten. Boston: Ginn and Company, 1935.

Burrell, Tom. *Brainwashed: Challenging the Myth of Black Inferiority*. Carlsbad, CA: Smiley, 2010.

Cannon, Katie G. "Slave Ideology and Biblical Interpretation." In *The Recovery of Black Presence*, edited by Randall C. Bailey, 119–28. Nashville: Abingdon, 1995.

CNN Report: http://ac360.blogs.cnn.com/2010/05/17/ac360-series-doll-study-research/.

———. http://i2.cdn.turner.com/cnn/2010/images/05/13/expanded_results_methods_cnn.pdf.

Cone, James. *Martin and Malcolm in America: Dream or Nightmare*. Maryknoll, NY: Orbis, 2005.

Bibliography

Council of Economic Advisors for the President's Initiative on Race. *Changing America: Indicators of Social and Economic Well-Being by Race and Hispanic Origin.*

Davidson, Karina, Bruce S. Jonas, Kim Dixon, and Jerome Markovitz. "Do Depression Symptoms Predict Hypertension Incidence in Young Adults in the CARDIA Study?" *Archives of Internal Medicine* 160 (2000) 1495–1500.

Davis, Reginald. *The Black Church: Relevant or Irrelevant in the 21st Century.* Macon, GA: Smyth and Helwys, 2010.

Douglas, Kelly Brown. *Sexuality and the Black Church: A Womanist Perspective.* Maryknoll, NY: Orbis, 1999.

DuBois, W. E. B. *The Souls of Black Folk.* New York: Barnes and Noble Classics, 2003.

Fleming, Chris. *Rene Girard: Violence and Mimesis.* Malden, MA: Polity, 2004.

Franklin, John Hope and Alfred A. Moss, Jr. *From Slavery to Freedom: A History of African Americans.* New York: Knopf, 2002.

Franklin, Robert. *Crisis in the Village: Restoring Hope in African American Communities.* Minneapolis: Fortress, 2007.

Girard, Rene. *Deceit, Desire, and the Novel: Self and Other in Literary Structure.* Translated by Yvonne Freccero. Baltimore: Johns Hopkins University Press, 1966.

Glasgow, Douglas G. *The Black Underclass: Poverty, Unemployment and Entrapment of Ghetto Youth.* New York: Vintage, 1981.

Glaude, Eddie, Jr. "The Black Church Is Dead. *The Huffington Post,* February 24, 2010.

Harris, J. E. *Africans and Their History.* New York: New American Library, 1987.

Harrison, Milmon F. *Righteous Riches: The Word of Faith Movement in Contemporary African American Religion.* New York: Oxford University Press, 2005.

Hine, Darlene Clark, William Hine, and Stanley Harrold. *The African American Odyssey,* 3rd ed. Upper Saddle River, NJ: Pearson Prentice Hall, 2006.

Kitwana, Bakari. *The Hip Hop Generation: Young Blacks and the Crisis in African American Culture.* New York: Basic Civitas, 2002.

Kunjufu, Jawanza. *Adam Where Art Thou.* Chicago: African American Images, 1994.

Leary, Joy Degruy. *Post Traumatic Slave Syndrome.* Milwaukee, WI: Uptone, 2005.

Lincoln, C. Eric. *The Black Muslims in America.* Grand Rapids: Eerdmans, 1994.

Lincoln, C. Eric and Lawrence Mamiya. *The Black Church in the African American Experience*. Durham, NC: Duke University Press, 1990.

Mamiya, Larry. "River of Struggle, River of Freedom: Trends Among Black Churches and Black Pastoral Leadership." *Pulpit and Pew*. Durham, NC: Duke Divinity School, 2006, 1–39.

Marx, Karl. *Contribution to Critique of Hegel's Philosophy of Right*. Translated by Annette Jolin and Joseph O'Malley. Cambridge, UK: Cambridge University Press, 1970.

McWhorter, John. *Losing the Race*. New York: The Free Press, 2000.

Mitchem, Stephanie Y. *Name It Claim It: Prosperity Preaching in the Black Church*. Cleveland: Pilgrim, 2007.

Muhammed, Dedrick. "Race and Extreme Inequality," *Institute for Policy Studies*, June 11, 2008: http://www.ips-dc.org/articles/454.

Nietzsche, Friedrich. *The Will to Power*. New York: Random House, 1967.

Pinkney, Alphonso. *The Myth of Black Progress*. New York: Cambridge University Press, 1986.

Price, Frederick K. C. "Ever Increasing Faith" program on TBN (March 29, 1992).

Raboteau, Albert. *Slave Religion*. New York: Oxford University Press, 2004.

Robinson, Eugene. *Disintegration: The Splintering of Black America*. New York: Doubleday, 2010.

Robinson, Randall. *The Debt: What America Owes to Blacks*. New York: Plume, 2000.

Shapiro, Thomas. *The Hidden Cost of Being African American: How Wealth Perpetuates Inequality*. New York: Oxford University Press, 2004.

Simmons, Martha. "Trends in the African American Church." *The African American Pulpit* 10:2 (Spring 2007) 9–16.

Tatum, Beverly. *Why Are All the Blacks Kids Sitting Together in the Cafeteria? And Other Conversations About Race*. New York: Basic, 2003.

Thompson, LeRoy. *Money Cometh to the Body of Christ*. Tulsa: Harrison House, 1999.

Thurman, Howard. *The Luminous Darkness*. New York: Harper and Row, 1965.

Washington, Joseph R., Jr. *Black Sects and Cults*. New York: Doubleday, 1972.

West, Cornel. *Race Matters*. Boston: Beacon, 1993.

Bibliography

Wilson, Amos N. *Blueprint for Black Power: A Moral, Political and Economic Imperative for the Twenty-First Century.* New York: Afrikan World Infosystem, 1998.

Woodson, Carter. *The Miseducation of the American Negro.* Chicago: African American Images, 2000.

———. "The Negro Church, an All Comprehending Institution." *The Negro History Bulletin* 3:1 (October 1939) 7.